WOODWORKING

The Complete Woodworking Tips and Starting Simple Projects

(Learn Fast How to Start With Woodworking Projects Step by Step Guide)

Donald Olivarez

Published By Donald Olivarez

Donald Olivarez

All Rights Reserved

Woodworking: The Complete Woodworking Tips and Starting Simple Projects (Learn Fast How to Start With Woodworking Projects Step by Step Guide)

ISBN 978-1-77485-383-2

All rights reserved. No part of this guide may be reproduced in any form without permission in writing from the publisher except in the case of brief quotations embodied in critical articles or reviews.

Legal & Disclaimer

The information contained in this book is not designed to replace or take the place of any form of medicine or professional medical advice. The information in this book has been provided for educational and entertainment purposes only.

The information contained in this book has been compiled from sources deemed reliable, and it is accurate to the best of the Author's knowledge; however, the Author cannot guarantee its accuracy and validity and cannot be held liable for any errors or omissions. Changes are periodically made to this book. You must consult your doctor or get professional medical advice before using any of the suggested remedies, techniques, or information in this book.

Upon using the information contained in this book, you agree to hold harmless the Author from and against any damages, costs, and expenses, including any legal fees potentially resulting from the application of any of the information provided by this guide. This disclaimer applies to any damages or injury caused by the use and application, whether directly or indirectly, of any advice or information presented, whether for breach of contract, tort, negligence, personal injury, criminal intent, or under any other cause of action.

You agree to accept all risks of using the information presented inside this book. You need to consult a professional medical practitioner in order to ensure you are both able and healthy enough to participate in this program.

TABLE OF CONTENTS

INTRODUCTION 1

CHAPTER 1: INTRODUCTION TO WOODWORKING 5

CHAPTER 2: DESIGN IDEAS FOR GARAGE CONVERSION ... 14

CHAPTER 3: TAKING CARE OF YOUR WOODWORKING TOOLS 27

CHAPTER 4: INTRODUCTION TO WOODWORKING WITH WOODWORK 32

CHAPTER 5: SAFETY FOR WOODWORKERS 39

CHAPTER 6: INNOVATIVE CREATIONS 43

CHAPTER 7: LEARNING THE BASICS 61

CHAPTER 8: MAINTENANCE OF TOOLS 68

CHAPTER 9: THE EASY CHAIR PROJECT 81

CHAPTER 10: HISTORY OF WOODWORKING 102

CHAPTER 11: SAFETY PRECAUTIONS 125

CHAPTER 12: TECHNIQUES FOR CUTTING DOVETAILS ... 130

CHAPTER 13: ADHESIVES 136

CHAPTER 14: IMPORTANT THINGS TO REMEMBER WHEN SETTING UP A WOODSHOP 142

CHAPTER 15: DIY PROJECT PLANS 147

CHAPTER 16: WHAT TO SET UP YOUR WORKBENCH 172

CONCLUSION 185

Introduction

My first experience with finishing furniture was a common experience to the majority of woodworkers. I employed brushes to apply varnish. The results were not the most impressive. Then, I found wipe-on finishes that produced more appealing results.

However, I found the process to be slow, and the finishes available are limited. Therefore, I made a decision early to study how to spray finish. Because I had had experiences with painting carriages I was familiar about the process and I was aware of how effective the outcomes could be.

After that, I began using a variety of air compressors as well as spray guns. Eventually I am now able to say I'm proficient at spraying finishes. As the path to becoming proficient was paved with drips and runs of paint, spray finishing was not much more complicated than other woodworking techniques that I've learned to master.

While many woodworkers have to struggle with brushes and rags I am able to say that I am happy to finish. The tools are enjoyable to use and I am awed by the outcomes.

Many woodworkers avoid spraying finishes due to fears of the need for additional equipment such as ventilation, overspray dust, the learning curves, etc.

However, the reality lies in the fact that one can survive using a handful of basic tools like a small compressor and an HVLP gun that is gravity fed as well as a cheap window fan, so long as you choose to use water-based finishes.

For solvent-based finishes, due to their flammability, they need to be applied using suitable explosive-proof light fixtures as well as exhaust motors. The only exception is when you are working outdoors and far from any ignition source.

In this guide, we'll begin by examining the steps needed to prepare for finishing projects how to prepare the surface, what are the different types of varnish and oil blends water-based finishes, the best way you can prepare your surface and the best application method. The next step is to examine the application of finishes made from water, the sanding methods hand-sanding techniques using tabletop flattening, and curvature shaping.

The next step is look at the benefits of spray finishing using the spray gun, high-pressure sprayers like HVLP spray systems , the vacuum-motor spray rigs spray guns for touch-ups and how to set up to spray, basic spraying and the best way to spray furniture.

The next step is to examine the thinning process and making sure that the right gloves are used for aerosol finishes and solvents precise yields from the technique priming and sanding, clear coating and rub-out, methods for painted finishing including filling and sanding glaze coating strategies, the use of glaze coatings and the best way to use wood bleach.

Then, we're going to go over polished finishing techniques, decorative finish techniques, stenciling methods, grainsing methods, French polishing techniques, marbling techniques, rubbing techniques and finishing techniques that protect.

We will then proceed to explore other tools and accessories need, how to choose an appropriate finish for protection and how to apply polyurethane, the best way to use shellac, and the best way to apply lacquer.

Finally, we'll explain how to complete the task with a hand, as well as some tips on the proper cleaning procedures and storage. If you're prepared now, let's start!

Chapter 1: Introduction to Woodworking

Woodworking is a fun and enjoyable way you can make individual and unique work of art. It's a craft that can be cultivated in time, allowing you to begin with a simple project and then grow into huge creations which can extend to other structures and houses. As you expand your perspective to think about what you can accomplish in the near future first, you must start with the fundamentals. This requires you to organize your work space first. In order to do this, you will need to be familiar with the equipment you'll will need to acquire to begin. Here are some important information that will assist you in your quest to begin your journey into woodworking.

The safety rules that every woodworker must to be aware of

Safety is the primary factor that woodworkers should be aware of before even picking up a work tool. Accidents while working with the tools you use are likely in the event that you don't adhere to the safety guidelines for woodworking which is why they are crucial to be aware of when you are woodworking for a leisure activity or even a career. Here are 10 important safety guidelines you must keep at all times:

Always wear proper safety equipment when you work within your workplace. This will safeguard your ears from noise-producing equipment like routers and surface planners. You should wear gloves that are latex all the times to protect your hands. Safety glasses are crucial for eye security.

Always wear the appropriate clothes. For instance, loose-fitting clothes are not recommended. Be sure the clothes are comfortable and are comfortable for your conditions and also protecting your body from harmful woodchips that may be thrown at you during your work.

Be sure to look for screws, nails and other metal items before you begin cutting wood.

Be sure to stay sober while you work in wood shop. Avoid drinking and using drugs since they increase the chance of being injured while using power tools.

Always work in opposition to the cutting tool. The majority of machines are made to work in the opposite direction to the cut wood. This can help avoid unexpected injuries.

Always disconnect the power before changing the blades. Remove every tool from power when you're finished with it. This is best when you only use one extension cord to power the entire workshop.

Make sure to use sharp bits and blades (instead of putting your life at risk by using the dull blade) always because they are more secure and provide better results.

Don't reach for the blade to remove the cut-offs. Avoid touching any blade that is moving until the blade ceases to move.

Beware of distractions of all kinds. Do what you're doing prior to focusing on the interruption.

Tools you will need for Woodworking

There will be a need for some tools to begin your journey in woodworking. You may add more as you improve your skills. The first set of tools you will need are cheap and basic, since their goal is to familiarize the user with them to help you understand what they can do for the woodworking task.

Make sure you have measuring tools the length of your project, cutting tools as well as tools for shaping other tools as described below before you are ready to begin.

Hand tools

The claw hammer has smooth, slightly rounded end head.

" Layout Square 6" Layout Square for marking the line of a square for an end cut. It can be used to rapidly mark an angle of up to 45 degrees and measuring up to 6 inches.

Chisels for cleaning debris from mortises and joints.

The retractable tape of 25' is a measures cutting lengths, or to mark the location of attachment to another board.

A way to tell whether a piece of stock is vertically or horizontally straight.

Nail Sets to sink head nails in a flush position or under the surface of the wood.

A knife that can be used to make an outline on an item of stock or making a clean-up of the mortise in a hinge.

A sliding bevel for duplicating angles.

Screwdrivers of various sizes and types.

Block plane to cut small amounts of wood from the stock. It is also useful for cleaning edges during the assembly.

Power tools

The power tools are equally crucial for those who are just beginning in woodworking. They can enhance the excitement of woodworking, even though there is a perception that they're costly and only utilized by most skilled woodworkers. However, this is not the case because you can locate a few essential tools to set up your woodworking workshop, which are inexpensive and durable. The most essential power tools to begin with are:

Circular saw.

The tablesaw.

A power drill.

The Jigsaw.

A compound miter saw.

A random orbital sander.

The router.

Woodworking machines

They are still tools for power, but they're not as portable as the standard power tool. Once you buy them and you'll need the space and make use of them. The most important ones are the following: --

Jointer.

Drill Press.

Surface Planer.

Band Saw.

Radial Arm Saw.

Adhesives

This is necessary in situations where you have to seal or join 2 pieces of timber without causing holes. When you make your decision you should consider what kind of adhesive you choose, whether it is water-proof or not, how quickly it will dry and whether you'll need to fill in the gap. It is best to begin with these suggestions steps:

PVA The most commonly used glue for woodwork. It can be found in the local shops. It is perfect for connecting projects, but it can get messy if you're not cautious enough.

Hide The Hide is a well-known kind of adhesive, too and is the best to utilize to avoid having to cause a mess while connecting your projects. It's easily accessible too.

Epoxy is either a resin or as a hardener. It's a fantastic adhesive to work with and the primary benefit is its waterproofness.

Polyurethane: This type of adhesive needs to be activated with moisture to be used. After it has been used it is able to dry very quickly and hardens creating a solid connection in the region it was utilized.

Cyanoacrylate: It is ideal to join hard parts. It is quick drying, so you don't have to wait long if you're trying to finish your project in a hurry.

Chapter 2: Design Ideas for Garage Conversion

It's feasible to construct furniture anywhere you want -- I've tried it in the attic and on a small balcony, but it's much more fun and simpler when you work in a place that is specifically devoted to woodworking. You don't need to load all your tools and projects at the end of the day , or operate around lawn mowers or bicycle, or even cars. It's good to know you don't have to be as difficult as you'd imagine to set up an entire shop. The three shops in this article are excellent instances of what could be achieved on a range of budgets. All three are separated from the home that reduces the quantity of noise and dust that can be heard in the living area.

It was obvious that I was losing a lot of my heating bills by letting air through the garage doors. Kits for insulation and weather stripping are available for doors that are in good condition, however, the doors that were rotting had to be removed. The issue was how I could replace them. I considered an insulation system made of steel doors but did not enjoy the idea of lifting an open roll-up door during winter and letting cold air through. Instead, I chose to change one overhead door with a standard walk-out door. This would make it easy to enter and provide a few feet of wall space that is needed. I constructed this structure by framing two of narrow panels that could accompany a low-cost, prehung entrance door made of steel. Each panel is comprised of a frame made of 2x4 and covered by CDX lumber (rated for use on the outside). The frame is stuffed with rigid insulation and then covered by drywall on the inside surface. To enhance the exterior I attached and glued pine boards to the plywood to give it the frame-and-panel appearance. Windows with corbels that were square below the sill created the appearance of an Arts and Crafts element that could be a perfect match for my bungalow style. The second bay I needed a different strategy. While I do not intend to park a vehicle in the area but I did want to have a door large enough for cars to pass through should we choose to decide on selling the home. I also like the idea having a big opening to accommodate equipment and lumber, as well as let in the sun on pleasant days. As opposed to a roll-up doors I decided to go with two open-air carriage doors. I was thinking that these doors could be more weatherproof and provide more insulation. The elimination of the garage door's overhead tracks will also provide me with additional headroom and allow for greater flexibility with lighting arrangement.

After receiving an estimate of $6,000 to make professionally designed doors I decided that I could build my own. I wanted my doors to be light well-insulated and extremely rigid to withstand sliding as time passes. Frame-and-panel construction didn't appear to be a viable option to complete any of these objectives. Instead, I went with an torsion-box style that is comprised of a solid wooden frame that has plywood on each face, much like the method in which a hollow-core doors are constructed. This will result in a sturdy structure with plenty of insulation space. I began with 1-1/2 -in.-thick poplar frame that was joined by stub Tenons. Long tenons don't need to be used and in actuality, biscuits could be used as all strength comes from wood skins. I used a dado knife to cut an half - in.-wide and 1-in.-deep groove into the frame components. I also utilized the dado knife to cut stub-tenons on the sides of the pieces to match the groove. The frame was then glued and was screwed into the Tenons. The cavity was filled with fiberglass insulation, and put plywood in place and then nailed it to the sides. This resulted in a very sturdy torsion box which should be able to withstand sagging for many years. The outer surface is made of 1/2-in. plywood and the inside is 1/4-in. plywood to to keep the weight down. I included windows and covered the exterior with plywood to help keep the weight down. I also framed the inside with 3/4 -in.-thick lumber to give it a frame and panel appearance like the other bay. The end result is 48-in.-wide doors that are lighter than a standard solid oak entry door and at just $450, is significantly less expensive than a custom door. I hung the doors using long strap hinges, which are sturdy and attractive. They were also simple to set up. The first step was to attach those hinges onto the door using the lag screws. Then, I put the doors on shims to ensure they were properly placed. With a consistent gap all around, I secured those hinges onto the frame.

I attached 2x4s treated with pressure onto the floor of my concrete, putting rigid insulation between them. The insulation I employed was the same thickness as the 2x4s, and so I placed the sleepers 24 inches. on center. Typically , a spacing of 16 inches. is recommended to stop the floor from sinking due to the weight of large machines. However, since rigid insulation has a good compaction strength, 24 inches. is adequate. After screwing the 3/4-in tongue-and groove plywood I put a 6-millimeter piece of plastic on top of the insulation, which acts as an insulator for vapors, exactly as Gibson suggested. I removed as much as I could from the workshop by filling up an eight-foot. in diameter by 12' feet. containers for storage, which I delivered to my driveway prior to building getting underway. The problem was that some equipment didn't fit in the container, which meant I had to build flooring in two pieces and move the equipment between the two sides. The installation would have been much easier in a shop that was empty however, I was able to complete the whole floor completed in just a few hours. The floor is now warmer and easier to sweep and is much gentler to my joints and feet.

The ceiling was a problem. I am a fan of the design and reflection of light from an enclosed ceiling. However, the ceiling's lowest joists was now just 7 1/2 feet. from my newly installed flooring made of plywood. The room felt tight and cramped. The first thought I had was to apply insulation to the roof's bottom but leave the ceiling's joists exposed. The insulation company said that I'd need to protect the insulation by covering it with drywall or plywood when the joists are open and I thought about raising the joists as well as closing the ceiling. I talked to an official from the building department in my area regarding my situation , and an engineer from the department suggested they could increase the ceiling's joists up to 2 feet. without causing structural issues. I've always considered the building inspector as something to be avoided for small home improvement projects However, in this case they proved to be a huge assistance. I'm a woodworker and the thought to raise the ceiling's joists somewhat scary. However, the actual process wasn't too bad. I could reuse the old joists by cutting each one at a while and nailing them to their new locations. One of the smartest things I did was to lease an unplugged Paslode framing nailer from my local home-based store. The ceiling in the end is an impressive 9 feet. Although the floor plan didn't expand, the space is more spacious and thanks to the addition of 1/2-inch oriented strand boards to the ceiling joists I've got some storage space that is needed over the ceiling. To gain access to that space, I put in an attic ladder with a fold-down design and wired up a light for the attic. To add insulation, I chose to spray the bottom of my roof using open cell foam insulation. Since my rafters were only 6 inches. deep, I managed to get an R20. However, since foam virtually eliminates moving air which scientists believe is the biggest problem in heat loss, the foam should be very effective. When it was time to replace the lights, I decided to make upgrading them. I replaced my three previous 8-foot. two-bulb fixtures for nine four-foot. four bulb fixtures. This was effectively doubling the amount of light that could be found in the shop. In addition to the white walls and ceiling my shop is now glowing.

The walls of frames are simple to insulate. However, the walls in my shop are concrete blocks which is why I chose an insulation method more suited to a basement store, however, with an updated twist. Instead of framing out this concrete structure in the standard manner with studs at the edge and insulation in between, I decided to take an alternative strategy. I began by covering the masonry wall in an unbroken layer of rigid insulation sandwiching it between two plates which I then nailed to the wall. Then, I sewed the studs in a flat position against the insulation before nailing onto the plates. Then, I put another layers of insulation on top, and was finished by putting up the drywall. Placing the studs along the edges could have resulted in thermal bridges from blocks to wall, thus reducing the insulation aspects that the walls have. The layer of insulation that continues that is between block walls and the studs creates a thermal break that will result in lower heating bills. The wall that is completed is 3 1/2 inches. thick but has an R-value that is over 20.

The project started out as an overdue insulation task ended up becoming a an entirely new workspace. The doors were replaced. I wasn't planning to improve my house and the result is a charming backyard store which is inviting and bright.

The shop isn't the only thing that's been renovated. I've also learned some new techniques. I've also done lots of framing work and remodeling. I've gained new skills in drywall and have a new appreciation for who are skilled at it. Basic wiring is not a problem for me. However, as much as I've been enjoying the new challenges, I'm glad to put my tools aside and return to woodworking.

If you're building a store and are concerned about its aesthetics or its resale worth the hiring of an architect is well worth the relatively small amount of cash. In my instance the architect came up with a variety of building options that would raise the ceiling, without raising the roof. He also convinced me -- against the advice of the contractor--to maintain the roof that had been bowed over the entrance door and he was available for any last-minute calls to resolve the inevitable issues that come during construction. Additionally, having full drawings of the plan allowed us to avoid an inspection agency that is often a burden. In the end, if I had to go through the process again, I'd probably have more questions for the architect, instead of the architect asking for. In order to make the building more resaleable we wanted the structure to be an garage for two cars, but we'll never put cars in it. On paper, something larger appeared like a huge structure in comparison to our modest house. The architect was able to ensure that the layout matched with our brick ranch home and drew an elongated hip roof similar to the one that is on the house. Then to stop the building from appearing like an unfinished box the front door with a tiny bump-out in a roof with a cantilevered. The architect was more concerned on the outside of his shop, I spent endless hours drawing the interior. I wanted lots of light as well as a spacious office and for waterstones as well as general cleaning, the convenience that comes with running water. I chose an unfinished toilet and a mop sink that has space for expansion later on and a tiny desk for books as well as computers. The two rooms are just 100 square. feet. of space. However, they can save me many trips to the home. With the bathroom and office at the back of the shop I ended up with 500 square. feet. of L-shaped space for the shop. Once we had a solid sketch, I created scaled cut-outs of my tools, and set them up. Before we began digging I needed to be sure that every item would be able to fit.

Chapter 3: Taking Care of Your Woodworking Tools

There are many things that are more fascinating than purchasing an all-new power tool! After saving the money while conducting the research and all the other purchasing, receiving the item and naming it your own is a great feeling.

Equipment: they're capable of cutting they're going to drill and to cut or flatten almost any thing. But, you must take care of these devices. Study and understand the user's handbook, and keep the handbook for future reference. After a device is set up but it needs to be regularly inspected for its the position, and for bolts that require tightening, lubrication, or cleaning.

Learn how to tune each gadget within the limits of the limits of its tolerances: band saw wheels need to operate in the same direction and a drill press needs to be able to lower and raise vertically in a square shape to its table and a table saw blade must be 90 degrees square to its tabletop, and its front and rear running along the miter slots. Books are a great source for information on this type of thing.

When you are packing an engine that is used for a lot of time allow it to grow to its maximum power so that it can complete its job efficiently. Newer devices, particularly need to be set to run for several minutes prior to heavy use the first time. This is to allow the brushes inside the motor to be able to 'seat.' Know the sounds of the motors on every device, and keep track of the sound it makes during operation. If there's a problem you'll often be able to hear or feel it on the device prior to anything going wrong.

Avoid working with any tool too fast. If a process requires more force than it should, it's a sign that something is probably incorrect, such as hardened wood or not enough clearance for a blade's chips or misalignment of crucial components. If you are concerned that the task is straining your device find a better approach, or break the work into smaller steps.

Know where your 'panic button Find out where your 'panic' button can be located. Make sure you are able to hold the workpiece free of the blade, and then switch the device off and on. Before starting, you must know the location of the off-switch, and know how you're going to reach it. There are after-market solutions to enable off-buttons to be accessible from your knees instead of having to search for them by hand.

Make sure to unplug the device whenever working with cutting or changing the blades. A bump to switches give you a unpleasant surprise but, damaged switches (even those with'safer' magnetic switches) are recognized to be connected and turn onto the table with a slam onto a tabletop, similar to an object that has fallen or a an object of wood. If you're experiencing power outages, unplug each device on its own and then leave the lights on in order to alert that the power has been restored back.

Keep your devices tidy. Clean the dust from the motor's vents and off belts pulleys, switches, and inside the router collets. Clean the band saw's tires with a toothbrush , and isopropyl alcohol. Turn the wheels with a hand. If you own rack and pinion height adjustment, ensure that the gears and teeth are free of sawdust.

It is a good idea to ensure that your workpiece is securely secured in place or oriented towards through a saw. Do not cut with a freehand blade using a table saw. help the workpiece by fences or miter gauges However, you should not use the two in conjunction because it may create a binding between the workpiece and the blade, triggering the blade to jam or kick back to the saw. A sled for cutting panels that is mounted inside the slot for miter cutting is the ideal way to cut cross-cuts. Utilizing portable power tools Before you begin think about how your electrical cable will flow smoothly as you complete the task, and make sure the cable is of adequate length (this is a major advantage of using battery-powered tools.) Make sure that the cable doesn't get caught onto something unnecessarily or wrap in your shoes. The most effective advice on new machinery is to educate yourself about it and then do some practice prior to starting your work. Woodworking is a great hobby, but you are responsible for your health.

Now you're prepared with the right tools. Let's look at some terms in woodworking that you might not know at the moment.

Chapter 4: Introduction to Woodworking With Woodwork

Before you can even begin to make an abrasion into your wood there are some points to be aware of during the entire procedure. The woodwork itself is so good as an person who designs the material from it. A solid foundation of knowledge prior to starting is essential. In this chapter, we will discuss all you require to learn to more comfortable with your woodworking.

This is The Stuff Good Wood is Made of

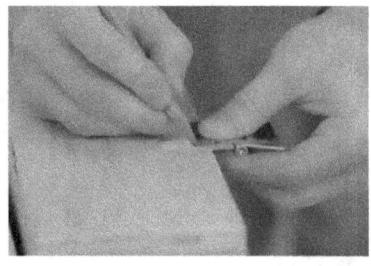

The wood is like a fine drink that is available in a myriad of flavors. And like good wine, it improves over time. There's wood that's suitable for furniture, as well as wood that is suitable for outdoor decks. There's wood that's suitable for Autumn, wood that is suitable for Spring, and wood that can withstand the most severe winter weather can bring.

With that in mind Here are some examples of different wood kinds and what exactly they are able to be used for in the woodworking project you are working on.

Pine

Pine is a softwood, which is malleable and is suitable to use in a variety of purposes. The color of pine is typically cream-colored, providing true light to indoor spaces. The material is a wonderful feature during winter, when a touch of brightness can be a great way to offset an otherwise dull and dark day.

Cedar

Easy to use and fragrant cedar can stand up to the pressures of the environment are put upon it. This is why that cedar is an ideal choice for furniture for your patio. Cedar is sturdy enough to withstand the stresses of the outdoors, but nevertheless pleasing to the eyes.

Cherry

Cherry is a wood that is also extremely sturdy and can withstand the elements. It is known for being resilient to rot, and solid and sturdy. It is, however, malleable in its structure and is able to be utilized for a range of or applications.

Redwood

Redwood is another great option for furniture that can be used outdoors and as the name implies, the wood is available in a gorgeous red color that people love on their decks and lawn.

Maple

In addition to producing maple syrup, maple trees also provide the perfect hardwood to build any type of furniture for indoor use that you might like to build.

Making the Right Choices with the Tools

Before you start your wood projects , it's crucial to have the appropriate tools for your task at hand. In the course of your woodworking, you might encounter heavy and lighter tools, manual tools or power equipment, as well as everything else in between.

Here's a list of the most essential tools you need immediately upon launching:

Measurer Tape Measurer

This could be one of the most essential tools that every woodworking enthusiast should keep in their toolbox. However, you can't accomplish anything without proper measurements, and a tape measurer will assist you in ensuring that you've got the right measurements. Instead of making an educated hypothesis, the tape measurement lets you break things into tiny individual intervals called"tic" "tic".

Power Drill

A power drill has become a standard and the mainstay of many DIY projects. It is as essential in all woodworking. The power drill is able to quickly cut through any type of wood, which can cut down the time spent on labor by a significant amount. Make sure you keep one in your arsenal.

Power Jointer

The instruments used are designed to smooth rough edges, and to make stylish curvatures. Instead of using the traditional method of using sandpaper. With the tool you will be able to swiftly smooth almost any piece of wood that you might own.

Manual Hand Saw

Hand saws are manual and an unassuming tool, however, it definitely serves some purpose. Because it's a handsaw that can be employed to cut chunks of wood which power tools could harm. This kind hand saw also happens to be quieter than other tools, which is why it should be considered for when you want to keep the volume in your shop at a minimum.

Get Your Wood Shop Get It Ready

In the woodshop, everything takes place. It's the location that contains all your tools as well as your wood supplies neatly stored away ready for your next woodworking venture. It is also the place where you store all of your safety gear. You must have things such as eye protection as well as first aid kits and work gloves that are within reach in case you require them.

Additionally it is essential to have a sturdy work bench. Its name could be misleading since the bench isn't designed to be used for sitting, but to be used for work. The bench must be well-constructed and have a working surface made of wood. It should be strong and mobile in the event of need. With the bench, it is recommended to be able to have a portable table close by.

With that traditional basic tool of carpentry the saw horse likely be a good idea, too. However, perhaps the most important aspect for your wood shop is to have a suitable location to store all the equipment mentioned above. That means you have to have enough cabinets, drawers, and other storage areas where you can store all of your belongings. Prepare your wood shop!

Chapter 5: Safety for woodworkers

Woodworking can be fun however, it can be hazardous also. Keep in mind that you'll work with power tools as well as heavy wood pieces. There are risks of accidents, so you must be aware of these safety guidelines:

Always wear safety gear.

This is the most crucial security rule you must adhere to. It is important to follow:

Safety glasses - These can protect your eyes.

The hearing protection will safeguard your ears.

The use of face masks could generate a lot dust, so it is important to ensure your face is protected.

The face shield fully face shield will shield you from chips flying around.

Dress in a professional manner.

It is essential to dress in comfortable clothes. This makes it easier for you to move around and carry things.

Connect the power source before making blades change.

Power saws can be dangerous Therefore, it is essential to turn off the power prior to when changing blades.

Don't use several extension cords.

To avoid electrical or fire issues, you should only make use of only one extension cord. This will prevent fires or electrical problems.

Use sharp blades.

Cutting tools that are dull are risky Make sure to keep your blades sharp.

Take care to organize your nails.

Don't let nails fall on the floor. Make sure your nails are neatly kept tidy every day.

FOCUS

To avoid accidents, it is important to stay clear of distractions and keep your eyes on the work that is at hand.

Your safety is the number one priority.

Tips for finishing and staining

It's easy to be attracted to cut your sanding project shorter. You may also be enticed to finish the prep work done quicker. Be aware that you shouldn't be doing both because these phases of woodworking are essential in order to create a the highest quality finish.

Reminders to finish and stain

Allow all finishes and stains to completely dry

Always test the finishes and stainings on scrap wood before you apply them.

Be sure to clean the lid of each can to ensure that the lid doesn't seal properly.

Make sure to clean the brushes before they are being used for oil-based finishes.

Always smooth the edges

Sand all surfaces prior to applying stain

Make use of mineral spirits on a damp cloth to wipe it down on your items

When you use maple, porous hardwood or softwood, you should coat the wood surface with wood conditioner prior to applying a finish or stain.

Take five to fifteen minutes to allow the wood to soak up the conditioner. Clean the excess off. This will ensure a smooth finish in the future.

Chapter 6: Innovative Creations

1. Mini Desk Masterpiece

Tools and Materials:

Pallets

Hammer

Nails

Stain

Saw

Sandpaper

Pencil

Measuring tape

Steps:

Step 1: Begin by removing all of the wood from one the side of the pallet. Take a measurement of your desk to determine where the stand will be, and mark it on the pallet the area you'll have to cut. Follow these lines using your saw, and then use Sandpaper to sand the wood until it's smooth.

Step 2 2. Apply a stain on the wood right now, giving the wood a natural look.

Step 3: Sand off the rough areas and then your stand is complete!

2. Rustic Pallet Wagon

Materials and Tools

Pallets

Hammer

Nails

Stain

Saw

Pencil

Measuring tape

Wheels

Rope

Steps:

Step 1: Begin by sanding the pallet. There shouldn't be any rough spots or splits in the wood. Apply stain.

STEP 2: When the stay is dry then flip the pallet over and use your pencil to mark the area you would like the wheels to go. Fix them securely.

Step 3: To make handling, I would suggest buying two hooks from the local hardware store and fix them just in entrance of the vehicle. The rope should be looped through the hooks and secure it. That's it! Your car is prepared to handle everything.

3. Quirky Office Desk

Tools and Materials:

Pallets

Extra poles for legs

Paint

Hammer

Nails

Stain

Saw

Pencil

Measuring tape

Steps:

Step 1: Take every piece of wood on one pallet , and cut the lengths in half. Attach them to the second pallet. Then sand the wood so that you don't have to fret about splinters.

Step 2: Ensure that there aren't any cracks or rough spots. After that, you can stain. Once the stain is dry then flip it over.

Step 3: Paint all four poles in the shade you prefer and set the poles in a similar distance on the bottom of the table. Fix the screws securely.

Step 4: Ensure that there aren't any rough spots and your table is now ready to play!

4. Practical Pallet Chair

Materials and Tools

Pallets

Hammer

Nails

Stain

Saw

Pencil

Measuring tape

Steps:

Step 1: Begin by disassembling the pallet completely. It is possible that you will need two So, go ahead and dismantle two.

Step 2: You are going to require 16 boards that measure 2 feet long, then cut them. You'll also require 4 boards that measure 4-foot long. two boards which are 3 feet long (cut these by bending the legs bent so that they be able to sit in the ground) and one support board.

Step 3: Sand all of these boards smooth, then arrange them in a grid. Take the image as a guideline and screw the 16 boards in an angle. They are the chairs' seats and you can screw the two sets of four-foot boards at right angles, and utilize the image again to determine where to put the chairs feet.

Step 4: Secure the entire piece to each other, and then apply stain. Dry, then put an additional cushion on top.

5. Super Slim End Table

Materials and Tools

Pallets

Hammer

Nails

Stain

Saw

Steps:

Step 1: This final table is very simple to construct. Cut a single pallet in the middle of each piece of support. Sand them down, and then apply a stain. Finally, stack them up in the manner shown in the picture.

Step 2: Spray a second stain, then screw it into the desired location. Allow to dry and then you're finished!

GARDEN furniture with wood PILLETS (BEGINNERS PLAN)

1. Pallet Garden Sofa

It is possible to create your own sofa with pallet to beautify your garden or patio. There are a few suggestions to design a pallet sofa

Materials and Tools

9 Pallets

Drill Level, Hammer, and Drill

Sandpaper

Saw and Nails

Paint and Paintbrush

Wood screws

Steps:

Step 1: Pick Up Your Pallet

The typical size of a pallets is 9 and you must select the finest quality pallets to create a sofas. There are some interesting wood burnt or stamped wood. It is crucial to look over some additional details.

STEP 2 Step 2: Cut Pallets

You must cut these pallets to 27.5 inches so that you can mix them effortlessly. It is possible to cut across the planks and take off a few edges on the 2 by 4 side. It is possible to make use of 2 by 4. By slipping into the opening and reattaching by using nails. The total length could be 78"x the width of 78".

Step 3. Create Cushions

It is necessary to cover the in the front gap of 2 by 4 of the pallet by using cushioning and mattress. You can make use of a few mattresses to make your own cushion since foam can be costly and you can also cut an old mattress to create cushions.

STEP 4: Secure the Backs

It is possible to use a few screws to join pallets and put them in the edge. It is recommended to use screws that are 2 inches long. It is possible to decorate your patio and utilize it as a seating area for parties or other arrangements.

2. Shelves to Garden

Materials and Tools

Sandpaper

Drill level, drill, and hammer

2 pallets of wood

Wood screws

Wood 2-by-4 inches

Saw and Nails

Paint and Paintbrush

Wall anchors

Steps:

Step 1. In the very first step, you must smooth your surface wood in order to

create smooth surfaces for the pallets. The underneath of the pallets.

STEP 2 The wood screws and the drills are employed to join the pallets. One pallet should be placed on the top of each one with the opposite direction. The lower sides will hold onto the shelves.

STEP 3: Determine the inside of the top pallet's its width. Cut the wood to a size of 2 inches by 4 inches. Install this wood horizontally into the pallet, and hold it at least 6-8 inches away from to the edge of the wooden. Verify for the proper level to be sure that it is level before placing it on the highest point of the piece of wood. Fix the shelf using the help of hammers and nails. Repeat this procedure for each shelf.

Step 4: You can make your shelves painted or left as is to create a rustic appearance. With the aid of anchors or wall studs you can attach the shelving unit onto the wall.

3. DIY Garden Chair

Tools and Materials:

Miter saw

Flat bar

2 wooden pallets

Nail puller

Box and stainless steel screws

Measurement tape

Screw gun

Steps:

Step 1: Pick up the pallet from the wood and put it level on the work surface with the highest surface facing upwards. The bar with a flat surface will slide underneath the first two boards on the other edge of the wooden pallet, and take them in a careful manner.

Step 2: Remove the nails from each pallet board using the aid of a nail puller. The pallets should be cleaned by taking off any nails that are drifted, and place the boards on their side. Repeat the process, and then remove nail heads from every of the boards and then cut the pallet boards to be used as to be used as the rear of the arm, legs, and chair.

STEP 3: Grab two wooden boards, and then measure out the 12 inch surface using measuring tape and a pencil. Cut with a miter saw to length of the front leg.

Step 4: Put the leg's end, which is in conflict with the boards that are separated in the pallet used for chair assembly and then move it upwards. Make sure you have one support facing forward to each side on the top and drive four screws of wood with equally space through the leg to the pallet's exterior by using a screw gun.

STEP 5: Set the second level of the pallet on the floor while maintaining the top one facing upwards. Remove the half-board from one side of the pallet and wash it by pulling the nails off using a nail puller. This pallet can help you build a seat. It is completed by removing the boards for the back legs.

Step 6: Place the pallet intended to be used as a back seat, by bringing the rear leg through four boards. Lower the back legs onto the work surface. use four screws to fix the seat. It is possible to use the screw gun to secure the joints of the chair.

4. DIY Coffee Table

Tools and Materials:

Drill

Hot glue gun

Stain or paint

The suitcase or the chest

Staple gun

Measuring tape

Legs and storage containers

Top plate hardware

Fabric or Velvet

Wallpaper

Trim or cording

Wooden dividers

Steps:

Step 1 Sand the woods of your pallet and paint them in accordance with the color of your chest. Examine the chest carefully and take off any fabric that is ripped for a neat appearance to the storage on your coffee table.

Step 2 Take measurements of the legs and prepare the legs to ensure they are in the right spot. It is possible to use machines to fix nails, and then use wooden dividers for small compartments. It is a good idea to embellish your wooden dividers by wallpaper.

5. Pallet Stool to use in the garden

Materials and Tools

4 pieces of lumber to create your stool's legs (3 in. thick)

Drilling and wood glue

4 inches thick of wood to make a seat

Chisel

4 large screws

Varnish

Upholstery and padding

Steps:

Step 1 Take measurements of the stool to meet your requirements and then choose pallet wood for the stool. Cut the pieces into various pieces of wood to create legs and a seats. The seat could be either square or round.

Step 2: Make holes into the seat to secure legs to the four corners and then insert screws into the four corners of your bar stool. Cut the legs down to determine the maximum height of your stool. ensure that these pieces are at least 3 inches thick. Be sure to keep the size of the four legs equal.

STEP 3: You could apply wood glue to the holes in the seat to secure it around the screw head. Carefully place the legs in the hole. Screw them in until you feel resistance, and then hold it in place. Remove any glue that has escaped and allow the stool to dry.

Chapter 7: Learning The Basics

Woodworking is an art form that combines art which includes elements from design into sculptures or carvings being created. It includes but isn't only limited to the following sets of abilities: carving, carpentry and joinery.

Although it is a predominantly male craft however, there are a large amount of women who are skilled also. If the person is able to demonstrate the necessary set of abilities (which in the main part, requires some muscle strength in the upper part of your body) If he or can begin to give an entirely new look to basic bits of timber.

Everything you can think of could be constructed with just a block of wood. It could be an armchair, a fixture in the wall, a ornamental carving, or furniture that is sturdy. There is no limit to the creativity that can be created by this project. Before you begin exploring the possibilities that one piece of wood can create make, it is important to learn the fundamentals first. Knowing these will ensure that the entire process is smoother and more secure.

The Selection of Lumber

As wood is the main material to be worked on in the woodworking industry (as the name implies) It is crucial to be aware of how to choose high-quality wood for your project. The first step can determine the success or failure of your project.

Prior to anything else it is imperative to look for indications of degradation or features or characteristics of wood which make it difficult to work with. Examine every inch of stock for any obvious imperfections.

Be sure to follow the Basic Rules of Safety

Like any other activity it is essential to follow the rules to be adhered to in order to protect yourself. As woodworking involves the use of a large amount of sharp, heavy-duty electrical equipment, make certain to take your precautions. The primary rule for security is to keep the equipment sharp by making usage of bench grinders, or preferably, sharpeners that are wet. This will enable the tool to maintain its sharp and concave tip. Additional safety rules should be discussed in chapter 4.

The Right Speed

Wood needs to be occasionally turned to achieve an ideal shape. But, "slower" does not mean more secure or more secure "faster" is not equivalent to higher efficiency. There is a suitable speed to turn wood. The safe speeds range between 500 RPM and the maximum of 4000 RPM.

The stock that is 2 1/2" or greater should be rotated between 750 and 1,000 RPM. Anything less that 2 inches needs to be turned twice as fast. speed.

In essence the speed at the stock to be turned is proportional to the dimensions of the timber. The bigger the wood larger, the slower the turn will be.

How to Place the Hands

Because the hands are the primary ones utilized in sports, the correct position must be maintained. In the event of a mishap, serious injuries can result. The most important thing is to grip the tools or the stock in such a manner that allows for enough control, while keeping your fingers away of the cutting edge.

Use the tool using the dominant hand, and keep the hand of the non dominant at the top of the rest. The non dominant hand should be placed in such a manner that the finger that is pointed to rest under the machine and on the side of the tool rest which is not in contact with the wood, while the thumb rests sitting on top of the device.

Check that the Tool is in contact to the Rest of the Tool

The tool rest must be used constantly to keep the limbs in good condition. The practice of freehanding is never recommended because it can be an invitation to catastrophe.

Make sure that your tool rest sits located 1/4 inch of the base. Also, make sure to place the device on the tool rest prior to placing it on the stock. Be sure to not set it away from the tool rest since this will cause less support.

Use the Bevel

The bevel is a second tool that lets you cut wood in certain angles. The proper position of the bevel is to be placed at the rear on the edge of the tool which is laid over the wood. By doing this, you can control the quantity of wood that is taken off at once and also stop the tool from becoming entangled within the wood and being caught in the grip of the user.

Increase with the Grain, It's Not Against It

This technique is referred to for its use in "cutting downwards." This means one must cut the wood away from the edges and then weave it toward the center, and not the opposite way around (a technique known by the name of "cutting upwards").

Scrapers Trails and Cutters Trail

Woodworkers using cutting tools must always hold the forehand (the hand that rests on the rest of the tool) over the rear hand (the one who grips the tool's handle). This puts the tool in the "leading" location. Scrapers however must be handled in a reverse direction. That means the front hand should be placed lower than the hand in the rear. This puts the tool in the "trailing" location.

Practice practice, practice, practice

Skills will only get better through a combination of practice and time. Many woodworkers begin with a sloppy and slow pace. However, with perseverance and plenty of practice, you will be able to create more refined and balanced results and develop advanced skills. In the beginning, you may only be able to design simple projects. After focusing on a couple of things, one could be able to produce more complicated outputs.

Keep in mind that the tool should be held securely and not "choking" the tool. The same can be learned and refined as time passes.

Chapter 8: Maintenance of Tools

The proper care for your tools is a must for a variety of reasons, but primarily in regards to the safety and wellbeing of the person who owns the tool However, it is important to ensure that your tools remain working as long as it is feasible. Different tools require different levels of maintenance, and this is dependent upon the number of moving parts and the kinds of blades. Sometimes, it's just as easy as talking something to a grinding stone occasionally, however at other times, maintaining the sharpness is a major hassle. When using other tools, it's about taking care that the power tools are cutting or drill in the right direction and true to their accuracy.

A lot of tools, including simple handsaws and screwdriver bits, come with a brief guide which outlines the best ways to care for and keep the tools. Because of the range of tools that are available, this manual cannot go deep into the particulars of each model or brand of each tool, however, it will offer general guidelines regarding how to take care of and maintain the tools. However, having a handbook of these smaller ones will help you solve an issue that you have with your tool.

Making sure that tools are used in the way they were designed to function is vital for not only ensuring their usefulness over time as well as keeping the user of the tool protected and secure through the duration of the tool's usage. If an instrument is misused it's not just dangerous it can also invalidate the warranty of the tool, assuming it was covered by an implied warranty.

Handsaw Maintenance

Maintaining handsaws' sharpness can be difficult However, in reality it's all about good habits and common good sense. First of all, like other metal tools, it is best to keep the saws inside a dry and dry environment, like an instrument chest or tool box. Silica or charcoal packs will help keep the enclosed spaces, like ones that are free of moisture and will prevent your saws from getting rusty. Another method to prevent the rust off your saw blades is spraying them with WD-40 when you've used them for a while, and you don't need to dry them off after applying.

If your saws come with wooden handles oiling them to prevent them from cracking or drying in humid areas will ensure that you don't require replacing the handles anytime soon. A boiled linseed oil suggested, but alternative oils can be utilized for example, Tung oil or orange oil. If the rust has already built up using razor blades, you can use 320 grit sandpaper for cleaning it up, moving through the entire longest length far away from where the handle is. Do not remove rust while when you are moving the saw widthwise and don't travel from spine to blade; always moving from "heel" which is the beginning of the handle and then to the "toe" or the flat edge of the saw. This is directly across from the heel. And don't sand or use a razor toward your body.

Maintaining the handsaw's handle in good shape is crucial to ensure you are able to trust with every pull out and pull backwards and without the handle breaking during the cutting. We've discussed keeping it in good shape with oil, however, when it is attached to the blade it will build up rust, which decreases its durability. To get rid of rust off the handle, take it off it and put a sharp blade or sandpaper with smaller grit by carefully removing only the holes that hold the handle in place on the saw. Apply oil to it, dry it off and reconnect it onto the cutting blade.

Hand Tool Maintenance

Hand tools are an essential item to keep in good condition. While they're only employed to perform precise work, keeping them in good working order will ensure this work remains accurate and doesn't lose its edge due poor maintenance. Hammers or saws, wedges and other small cutting or whittling tools should not be left without protection when not in use. Keep them in storage as soon as you can and in a controlled environment. Sharpening hand-tools that require sharpening for sharpening, like planes and wedges, can be accomplished by hand, using the help of a grinding stone. If the handles start to lose their sharpness, think about replacing the item if cheap or repairing or replacing the handle if it's an expensive tool.

Press Maintenance Press Repair Drill presses may be more complicated than they appear, however they are still maintained. is not difficult. In order to keep a drill presse running well, there are numerous tasks to be completed, but they're all fairly straightforward.

First, lubricating the chuck, which is the jaws that close to grasp bits, is crucial in order to ensure that they be closed tightly to the bits. Clean the chuck and fully open the jaws. Blower out any wood chips or dust using a puff of compressed air. Wear glasses to avoid getting into your eyes. Examine the chuck to ensure that it is clean before moving on. After the chuck has been cleaned of any excess material, spray tiny amounts of lubricant upwards and down into the chuck, making the jaws move in the chuck while spraying. The excess lubricant will fall out, leaving the grasping mechanism that is smooth and easy to turn. Polish away any remaining grease and you're ready to go.

Once this is completed the next step for examination is that of the power cable. Check your cord has been secure well on both the machine-side and socket-side, and look for cracks, cuts or holes within the cord. If there are any you can repair the cord using the use of a rubber sealant or replacing it entirely.

To make sure that the drill is operating in good functioning condition, one has be sure that the machine is actually drilling. There are many aspects that affect the accuracy of the way the drill is tunneled The most basic of these can be the angle the point where the bit is inserted that should always be at least 90 degrees. to the most difficult issue, which is a drill that is not aligned. This is a problem that can be fixed at home, but. One of the first things to look for after making sure the bit is correctly installed and inserted, is to ensure that your drill is properly set up. If the drill is tilted in its set-up it could impact the level at which it drills.

Band seen Maintenance

The most important thing to learn about maintaining a band saw immediately is the need to "break into" blades. The process of breaking in the blade of a bandsaw will ensure that it stays sharper for a long time. When new, band saw blades are too sharp for everyday use they crack and break at tiny levels if they are not properly taken care of. The best solution is to cut less frequently in the initial 50 inches of usage. Slower cutting does not mean cutting down on the band saw's running speed. The blade should always operate at the same speed, however, it means that you feed the wood at a slower pace roughly half as fast as it normally does. There is no need to find precisely how long every cut you make however, you should try to keep for the initial 50 in of cut at half pressure. If you're not sure regarding the pressure you should use make sure you test it out and move the wood at a slower speed. As you progress to work on the blade you'll be able to be able to recognize the normal pace of cutting, as well as how you must be cutting when you break in a brand new blade.

Clean regularly your band saw's blade and bench. The bench should be free of rust and sawdust is advised. Simply brush off any sawdust with the wire brush, then get rid of rust using the razor or chemical cleaners. To cleanse the blade, turn off the machine and take out the plastic band saw's side cover. Then, remove the band out of its wheels and the housing. The blade can be polished by using a mixture of the resin removers as well as cotton cloth. This prevents the blade from being clogged by resin, which could be able to sit upon the edge and cause it to shake or move around inside its housing, which can cause damage to the machine. When the blade is taken out the housing you may use the same resin remover to clean the wheels the same way you applied it to the blade. The blade can be soaked in an soapy solution to wash it is also acceptable as it is done with care to ensure that it doesn't get rusty.

Sanding Tool Maintenance

Handheld sanding machines function in similar fashion to power tools work, however there's plenty to say about the maintenance of belt sanders. The most basic suggestion for maintaining the belt-sander's condition is regular maintenance of the sandpaper it self. They usually last for a long time if properly used, which means that you don't press too much into the tool while you sand. It is possible to use a amount of force, but make sure you don't overstretch or bend the sandpaper while you work. Keep the motor clear of sawdust in the best way you can. Also, regularly empty the bin for sawdust that is attached to many belt sanders. If the belt sander you have been fitted with a vacuum tube you should put an air hose through the tube throughout the use on the belt.

Power Tool General Maintenance

Power tools are, generally the same motor configurations that can be taken care of with the same manner. Some signs of damaged or used machines can be fixed quickly, while other issues will require the assistance of a specialist.

Power tools make use of brushes, solid blocks made of carbon that transfer electrical energy to the motor. They wear down over time, and you'll be able to be able to tell when they're worn by the time you start to notice visible, but non-threatening sparks in the power tool after usage. For the majority of modern power tools the brushes are quickly replaced. One can identify whether this is the case with their particular tool by identifying two black covers that are on each side of the motor housing. They are also known as the cap for the brush. If they are on your device replacing the brushes is easy as buying a new pair of brushes from the tool's manufacturer and then removing the caps and the brushes prior to replacing the caps. Be aware that as you loosen the caps of your brush and the springs that are in the brushes could cause the cap to snap loose, so prepare for this by inserting your finger inside the cap when you remove it and then gently remove it.

When your tools come with removable blades, remove the blades prior to storing them, and store the blades in an additional, humidity-controlled environment. This will help keep your blades free of rust and also prevent the tool from securing itself to the blade. It will also make sure that you are able to easily replace or remove the blade later on.

Cleaning the air vents by spritzing them with pressurized air can also keep the power tool run effortlessly and effectively for long durations. Be sure to not maintain the same spray while you go about this because of the nature of the pressurized air cans. Utilizing short bursts of air and increasing the speed of your motor in order to shift it around can help to achieve cleaner airflow.

Check the screws and fasteners fixing the casing of the tool, since they may be loosened by the force from the instrument itself. Make sure to tighten the screws frequently and, if you are unable to locate or use an appropriate screwdriver head, then take the tool to a local hardware store and speak to an employee to purchase the appropriate screwdriver or drill that is compatible with the specific type of screw.

Two issues that always coincide is the maintenance of tools and the use that is safe for tools. Utilizing tools in a safe manner is the best way to learn how to keep them in good condition, however, the proper use of tools is a complicated.

Chapter 9: The Easy Chair Project

This e Easy Chair is an excellent job to study the fundamentals of keeping things simple. If your uprights shift in length or if your horizontals aren't flat, you're likely to notice the seat rests. It could be

Even more, it's likely to be lacking the enthusiasm that will make you want more than sit.Since the process of studying and recalling fractions can cause trouble for all of us students, I'll demonstrate some easy methods to help you eliminate measuring. It will be possible to figure how to make use of clamps and blockages in order to reduce multiples by a exact same time and the fundamentals of glue-and-screw structures, how to make and utilize simple jigs to find joints, as well as how to use and keep the oiland varnish mixture in a complete way. The seat has twisting joints that are reinforced by glue. The screws provide the joints' foundation of strength. They also function as movements to keep the joints together as the glue is drying (you're still working with the clamps the position). The best seat for this is constructed with a tough watertight glue that is extremely flexible. It fills in gaps between finished joints, resulting in an extremely strong and watertight connection which is stronger than wood.The flexible glue-and-screw connection is an important improvement to your existing collection It can be utilized in various scenarios. You can leave the screw heads in view to create a simple and clean design (for example Jigs, for instance) or fill them with putty, or can pay for them with beautiful wooden strings that are inserted flush into the surface. A strong joint is a part of the reason this seat comes to last. The power redundant is integrated into the design.

Construction of the Chair

Before you begin making your plans, be sure to declare the timber with a sticker for a couple of weeks, according to the preceding chapter. This is especially important in the case of two 2s used as decking (meranti Ipe, meranti and certain cedars). The decking timber can be stored outside, which provides it with an increased moisture content. If not properly stored and treated the timber could be twisted and bow in the course of construction or shortly after. It is best to deliver the wood at your local store and then remove the pieces that become too bent from the process.

Create the Side Assemblies.

Once your wood has been prepared, you're ready to go. The first step will be to cut each of the 2 pieces to the appropriate length. Sanding and cutting foundation elements

By following the procedure described in"Skill Builder: Crosscutting Multiples into the same length" on page. 156, cut two 2s into 17 equal pieces approximately 24-" long (you require 14 for the seat , and the three other pieces are accessories for jigs, errors and other jigs). If you're using miter saws and your pieces are likely to be a bit smaller then 24". A

chop saw has a more robust blade that also produces more kerfs; the bits will likely be the same as 2315/16". It doesn't matter how they are as long as you ensure they're identical. Do not think that you'll be capable of cutting your entire 4' two 2s in half in one cut. If they are altered in length, in any way they will not emerge.

perfect? For security, position the block so that it is by less than". The first block should be cut in order to span the block, and then place another piece against the block. Finally, cut a piece of it.

Sand all four elements of each piece using an orbital sander, as well with 150-grit glue.

Figuring out from the stretchers

Start by crosscutting additional (or only one cut that is too quick) two 2s to make two equal pieces of 83/4" extended to make measuring cubes. They are much better than measuring tape for many"measuring" procedures.

Set two 24" pieces on the seat and then flush the ends by pushing them into one of the measuring cubes. Fix them in place to avoid shifting while establishing the uprights' positions.

Utilizing a measuring cube, as like in the photograph C, draw a line within the border. Set the block up and then set another one up.

block within the middle of these stretchers. Mark the block across

the inside border of this cube's outer border. Then, lift the block. create hatch marks on each line. This is the point where the spine crosses the stretcher. Then mark the end to the stretchers"Back"

With a ruler, mark marks on the rear end of the third vertical to the middle of the stretcher 9" on the horizontal line that corresponds to the back edge of the vertical at the rear (the very first line that you sketched in the previous step).

Note the position of their first vertical back at to the rear of the stretcher using the measuring block, as well as making hatch marks as in the second step.

Indicate the location of the next vertical 1 block-width to the right of the first vertical. To make the marks, then put the block on top of the marks made in step 5. Then put the second block on the inside of the first. Keep it in place

Mark the border of your interior. Don't take it off however.

Lift the first block, and then leapfrog it to the next one, and then place it in a snug position against the inside in the second cube. Let go of the leapfrogged block and hold the other one in place, and mark the border of the interior. Lift it off to

place hatch marks beneath it.

The uprights will be positioned from there.

The uprights grow under the stretchers and are extending in the width of a single block.

Twist four uprights with the end of the uprights flush and then clamp them as you did with the other stretchers. (it is easier to align everything four uprights at once instead of the eight at once)

Install an measuring block flush with one of the uprights. Then create a mark on inside of the cube along with the uprights.

In the absence of transferring the measuring block first, take another measuring block and mark the border. The space beneath the block is the place where screws pass through the vertical, and then to the stretcher. Mark every slice as"Upright."

Counter-insinking that the uprights are for stringing

Countersinks are nothing more than a funnel-shaped gap that matches the form of the top of the twist head. The countersunk holes allow the twist to sit to the timber's surface. If you countersink enough and the gap is large enough beneath the surface that it can be used to insert the wrought iron plug. It's a stylish method to hide the screw heads that are not attractive when working.

Begin by hanging the top part of your workpiece from the seat to ensure it doesn't get drilled into the seat.

Countersink and drill a little smaller than 1/8" thick (roughly 7/32") from the area where you have marked the hatch.

Attaching the uprights onto the stretchers

To keep the seat from shifting The uprights must be placed directly on the ground and the distance between the floor to the stretcher should be exactly the same for each. A simple jig created from a two-two is a simple way to set the uprights and keep the uprights in place as you fix them. (For more information on the jig, visit"Upright Jig" on page. 160.)

Set one stretcher over the seat, and then clamp it from the front to right. This is crucial. Negative assemblies aren't the same thing but they are

Mirror each other's images. If you follow the steps to reverse the hand, you'll be putting its opening on the left. Put an extra portion of two around twenty" across the stretcheder in order to support the uppermost uprights remain in place as you work.

Apply the paste on the stretcher, as well with regard to the back of the vertical in each counter-sunk hole.

Place the front vertically and the stretcher, using all the surfaces that have been glued. Use the jig to locate the correct position, and clamp to the required degree.

Two 21/2" screws into those holes that are countersunk. Make sure not to push the screw too far. If required, adjust the clutch so that it works properly. Examine the joint to ensure that the twist is through the entire way and that the two bits pull together so that the glue flows out.

Repeat steps 1 through 4 weeks until the second or third party and the rear uprights.

Place a second stretcher onto the seat, with the front facing your left. Attach the uprights to the frame as described earlier.

Attach the Side Assemblies with the Lower Crosspieces

Once you've put together the two sides and are ready to join them with the crosspieces of a smaller size. They connect the stretchers.

The foundation of the structure. Working out the crosspieces the two sides are held to each other using five crosspieces. The crosspieces extend 1 1/2" over the top of the uprights. This gives the chair a sense of visual.

1. The ends of the five crosspieces and make sure they are flush. Make use of your slipping squares to mark down lines at each end of the five pieces that are 1/2" to the left of the ends.

2. Take a look at the crosspieces. Two of them join the stretchers together at the stage where two blocks measure are removed from that line in Step 1. Let's call these Crosspieces of Sort A. Two additional crosspieces also have mouths, one measuring block that is straight and the other in the center of the mark. This is what I call Form B. 1 crosspiece, Form C, demands no additional mark. Utilize these

cubes to "quantify" these distances like you did with your stretchers and verticals and horizontal marks on the

Joint locations.

The crosspieces are counter-inked, so that they can be countersink.

If you have drilled countersinks out of the hatched regions around the uprights, repeat the process using the hatched areas of the four crosspieces. The fifth crosspiece does not have openings at present.

Connecting three crosspieces together to form one side

Set one side of the body onto the seat in a way that the stretcher is at the top with the extended underside of your thighs running along into the side of the chair. Place it in an elongated vise, or use us

in straps. Place the garbage or other crosspieces on the seat to hold the ends on the crosspieces.

Choose one Form A crosspiece to secure between the two uprights leading, set with the countersinks up.Apply paste to the floor and sides of the area that is over the crosspiece as well as to the mating surfaces on the other side that are gathering. Fix it to the ground as you press two 2-1/2" screws.

Similar to the crosspieces of the spine that are smaller glue it and place it on the back edge of this third vertical.

Remove the meeting from the vise, and place it on the benchtop. then secure the opposite hand and securing it into the stretchers. Check that everything is in line and you have a 1/2" overhang is set.

The ht is square, and the intersection is square. Next, clamp the top rear crosspiece to the set-up.

Eliminate the crosspieces , one at a time , and then inject epoxy into the mating surfaces of the stretchers, crosspieces and uprights. Once again, clamp set up (double half of the" acrosshang) and then push screws. Next, move to the lower crosspiece. At the end, fix the spine crosspiece on top.

Set up the Seat Supports

The supports for the chair connect to two side assemblies near the middle of the arrangement.

Installing the support for the rear seat.

Set a measurement block on the stretcher, in the side of the third vertical. Make sure to use one for each side and clamp them into their place (just 1 clamp is sufficient).

required).

Place the remainder of the Type B crosspiece beneath the measuring cubes and adjust. Put epoxy on the mating surfaces, and then turn the crosspiece that was to set it up. Take with care.

Fully preserving the half" overhang.

Take the measuring blocks out and wash them using alcohol. Then wash off any squeezes that are combined.

Supporting the front of the chair

A measuring block is placed underneath the lower front crosspiece that is affixed to the first and the next uprights.

Set the only Form C crosspiece beneath the cubes. Set up the clamp and countersink 2 holes each side of the front vertical as well as in the crosspieces.

Remove the front chair crosspieces to remove dust and dirt that is accumulating around the joint. Apply glue on all mating surfaces.

Replace the front chair crosspiece by carefully aligning the 1/2" overhangs. It is difficult to do this without spreading glue around however, do everything you can to reduce the mess to an absolute minimal. Take the screws out, remove the cubes, then wash them.

Set up your Back as well as Seat Planks

The 1/2" gaps between each board allows for the chair with air and keeps the water and leaves from collecting in the chair. Install the center plank , and then the sides are covered with

Then there's a little 1/2"-heavy garbage.

Cutting the seat and back boards

Crosscut three of the rear boards from 1by6 stock up and long 48" long.

Crosscut the three chairs boards from 1by6 stock up to 171/2" long.

With a random-orbit sander, along with 150-grit discs. Smooth the surfaces of the boards prior to bringing them together.

Installing the back board in the centre

If your workplace has lower ceilings, you may require moving your chair to the floor for the following steps. If you've got 50" above your workbench Keep the work on the chair and save your back.

With the aid of a tape measure, you can mark the and locate where the middles are of lower and top crosspieces at the rear, as well as the their front and back crosspieces.

With a ruler, draw an area half the length of 1 by 6(that is 23/4") from the centerline of each side. The edges of the center boards will be aligned with the lines.

Scrape two pieces two pieces of scrap under the seat to ensure that the bottom border of the plank could break. Make use of clamps to gently grasp the plank to the top crosspiece. The photo N shows the mark in step two as well as the extra bits that run fore and behind between the bottom of the plank as well as the seat.

On the back on the back of the panel, trace lines along the lower and top borders of the crosspiece supporting the upper part which will reveal the location of the adhesive. Similar procedure can be done for the lower spine's service crosspiece.

Determine the locations of the screws that could be used to attach these boards onto the upper and lower back crosspieces for service. Sit in seating area in front and bend to ensure that the upper back service crosspiece reaches eye level. Draw a smooth line with a pencil on the board, which appears to be the top on the end of the crosspiece. It's a good idea to countersink and drill for screws below the on the internet. You can do the same with your lower back option (if the seat you are sitting on is located on the ground, it is uncomfortable).

Get rid of the plank. Also, make use of an angle rectangle to trace vertical lines about 1/8" underneath the lines you drew by eye. This extra thickness protects of the angled ribbon not being used or coming from the crosspieces' border.

Note the locations of three holes, one on the center of the piece, and one pit 1" to the left and right of each edge. Drill and countersink screws to be placed around the lower and upper crosspieces.

Apply epoxy on the mating surfaces. Replace the middle plank with the traces, to get it a position. Apply the clamp gently. Make the first screw into the top countersink, and then examine the work on the surface. Are you sure it is rectangular? Is it able to be changed? Reposition the board as needed, then push the screw on the left corner countersink. The board isn't able to change, and you can push the remaining screws to nearly every purchase.

The side plans are being installed.

Remove the 2 by 2s away from the middle plank, so to support the bottom of the optimal plank. Place an 1/2" spacer that is twelve" long between the boards, close to the center of the trunk. set a cone over three bits , each

boards and the spacer. Insert another spacer in the base and secure it the boards, too. Make lines across the top of the rear crosspiece on each edge of the board, so that you are able to quickly duplicate it later.

Remove the plank, apply epoxy on the mating surfaces, and reclamp. Then, anchor the plank in the desired location.

After you've had some instruction it's possible to cut a few inches off the installation of the left hand side of the board. Apply the adhesive, then clamps, and the spacers, then move the attachments.

The installation of the chair boards

For setting up the chairs, you must follow the same procedure as all springs, however with one major change. If you were using those measuring blocks in order to keep the planks in the rear from the ground, you'll use a little of 3/4"-heavy trash to act as a gap between the chair boards and rear planks.

Set the centre board to the symbol 23/4" in the center with being a 3/8" gap between it and the chair, along to the back.

Drawing with your eye Draw a thin pencil line along center of crosspiece. Mark screw holes in mid-point and one" at each end.

Make use of half" spacers to position the side boards in the proper distance away from the central plank. You can also use the 3/4" spacer to position them in relation to each other.

Fix and glue in exactly the same manner like the rear planks.

Chapter 10: History Of Woodworking

The woodworking and human history is remarkably similar to that of time. From the time that people first were standing on two feet and started walking upright, the use of wood was crucial in the development of tools for survival, specifically to hunt and build homes. Apart from the mud, stone and animal parts wood was definitely one of the first substances with which primitive people used to work. Additionally, the development of the society is directly related to the improvement of capabilities in the work of these materials.

If we are looking at the past of furniture, we need to consider the smallest neolithic settlement located in Orkney the northwestern part of Scotland.

Skara Brae is comprised of eight homes that are connected to each other between the years 3200-2200BC via several passages. Each of the houses has remarkable surviving cabinets, beds with changing rooms, beds, and shelves. The sole reason they survived which makes them among the oldest furniture pieces around the globe was due to the fact that Orkney was not home to (and did not have) trees. The furniture of in the Stone Age is made entirely from stone.

Maybe not comfy, but it demonstrates the way furniture designers have created furniture for more than 4000 years. It's not a surprise that we had comfy beds, tables and chairs. We had the fundamental designs that have been used for centuries.

The Genesis Book depicts one of the first woodworkers of the world. God granted Noah the responsibility of creating an Ark constructed from cypress with the length of 300 meters 50 and the height of 30. This implies that the Ark could have been approximately 350 meters long and about the dimensions of a four-story structure should it ever be built.

Also, we should not overlook Saint Joseph, patron saint of woodworkers, as well as Jesus the father of Jesus. Of course, Joseph was an apprentice carpenter. But at the time the fathers were required to instruct their kids in the trade by twelve years old. Thus, Jesus would have been a furniture maker.

The truth is that the form of furniture has been in use since the beginning of time. The antique woodwork made by Egyptians, Greeks, Romans and Chinese can be seen. For instance in Pompeii archaeologists discovered an unremarkably clean furniture store that was destroyed by Mount. Vesuvius around 779 AD.

Wood has always been the most valuable assets of ours and is relatively simple to transform into tables and chairs. What has changed throughout the years is our capability to use wood in a more efficient way, with modern machinery and equipment taking most of the work done by donkeys away. The technology is still affecting woodworking. For instance;

3D printing or computer-aided design in which a specific design is built in miniature form for a single piece of mobilization and presented to clients to finalize design approval.

This is a highly-tech item which would have been aplauded by Noah. It could have saved Noah many headaches and could have given the unicorns the chance to rest.

Wood has been utilized by people for thousands of years to make useful, beautiful and attractive artifacts.

For the ancient Egyptians and for the Jews, Romans, Greeks as well as all the other Early Civilizations, woodworkers were essential to society over 2000 years in the past. The majority of images depict wooden furniture such as benches, beds, stools, benches tables, chests, and tables.

Here are some interesting information about these former woodworkers.

Early Egyptians also built wooden coffins.

In the Early Egyptians invented the art of furnishing Semekhet's tomb who died around 5000 years ago, and with the first examples. A lot of Pharaohs' tombs were decorated with pieces from African ivory and ebony inlays.

There are some scientists who claim that the Egyptians were the first to varnish (or "finished" wooden work but nobody is aware of the exact nature of these "finishes" are.

The ancient Egyptians utilized mortise and Tenon joints to join wood. Dowels, pegs, and leather were used to reinforce these joints.

Between 1570 and 1069 B.C., Egyptians started to make use of glue made from animals.

In the early days, Egyptian woodworker employed knives, adzes, chisels as well as pull saws and bow saws.

In the early Chinese civilizations woodworking was also promoted. Woodworking is believed to have been a major source of income for the world since approximately 720 B.C. At the time it was the time when the Chinese created a variety of advanced woodworking techniques. These included the essential steps for making tables, bowls, and various other furniture.

Woodworkers who use traditional methods of woodworking from the past are proud of their correct articulation and the ability to hold their pieces in place without the use of any electrical devices or glue.

Japan is the country where this style of woodworking originated in the majority of.

Another reason why Japan has managed to create with such a high-quality wood is the fact that it made high carbon steel tools in the early years of its development.

Japanese woodworkers also produced stunningly designed landscapes. The popularity of Japanese woodwork and its techniques were widely used throughout South-East Asia.

If a carpenter needed wood, he cut wood into boards with the help of others by using a massive bronze saw. He made thin boards out of the trunks of the trees. However, the trees that grew in that field were not particularly tall or straight.

Sage briefcase, adze line and plummet and rulers, chisel, adze, briefcase, stick, flat and squares were some of the tools used by carpenters that were mentioned in the earliest sources. They also employed the bow cooker, which was held with one arm by the handle, and then pushed it quickly by pulling back and forth on the gun.

The bowl was a primitiveand basic tool, yet skilled woodworkers could make attractive bowls and spindles similar to those used today in woodturning. The wood was turned around like an arch by pulling a strap made of leather. Its spindles moved his lath around and let it be cut through the rotting wood.

The woodworkers from the Near East built large wooden vessels from timber, which was developed throughout the Levantine Coast (the Mediterranean coastal land of modern Turkey, Syria, and Lebanon) within the Anatolian Plateau. This wood was so sought-after that it was frequently sought as a gift by invaders armies.

Archaeologists found furniture made from wooden pieces inlaid with bone bronze, or ivory dating to the 800th century B.C. The site of the alleged birthplace of the mythical King Midas in Gordion. The woodworkers of the Near East used lathes as well as maillots, wedges as well as hammers, chisels and chisels boxes, as well as other basic tools.

The windows made of wood of the first mosques as well as private homes that are evident in Arab culture were built during the height of the ancient wooden carvings throughout the Near East. For floors, walls rooms, rooms, and all sorts of furniture and fittings they Muslim carvers of Persia, Syria, Egypt and Spain have designed and made beautiful paneling and ornaments. The woodwork they created was intricate and tiny.

Woodworkers from the past were recognized for their skills and creativity, which laid the foundation for modern woodwork. Each of the tools we use today evolved from tools of the past like lathes, chisels and saws.

The process of woodworking also originates from those old craftsmen and the feat they achieved using 'primitive' tools is astounding.

As important to our society in the same way as timber is to our culture, wood can be overlooked or even forgotten. As technology advances, the technologies for space-age are being developed and the metal's use is becoming more well-known than ever. Metal is a natural resource at the heart of many things that we do as well, so take a look how it functions through the decades.

The firewood that was worked from Kalambo Falls, Clacton-on-Sea, and Lehringen were among the first discovery of instruments made from wood. One of the first examples of hunting gear made of wood are spears found in Schoningen (Germany). The cutting tools made of Flint were employed. Since the Neolithic period graven wooden vessels were recognized, such as in the Kuckhofen and Eythra Linear Pottery cultivation wells. The bronze age comprises trees that were made to be the northern German as well as Danish coffins as well as wood folding chairs. The Fellbach-Schmieden area in Germany has provided gorgeous examples of Iron Age wooden animal statues. Wooden idols from the period from La Tene are recognised in France from a sanctuary located at an area that is the origin of Seine.

The Egyptians as well as Chinese and the Chinese are two of the earliest civilizations who used woodworking. Woodworking is depicted in many antique Egyptian paintings. Significant amounts of Egyptian antique furniture (tools chairs, tables, chairs beds, and boxes) were stored in the tomb. The cassocks inside the graves were constructed from wood. It is believed that the Egyptian metal used to make woodworking was most likely copper, and bronze, which was used as ironwork. was not discovered until more than 2000 BC. The tools used for woodworking were commonly used as torches, adzes screws, chisels, or bow casings.

It also suggests that the first Egyptians constructed boards for ship hulls before 3000 BC. Shipbuilding has evolved into an important art since the very first wooden boats which helped in the movement of people along with commerce, and obviously war.

Chinese woodworking progenitors include Lu Ban and his wife, Lady Yun. Lu Ban's vessel, his chalk line, and various other tools are believed to have been brought to China. The lessons he learned are said to be preserved in the work that was written by Lu Ban Jing, although the book was written approximately 1500 years after the death of Lu Ban. The book is primarily a description of the measurement used to design various items (flower bowls chairs, altars and so on.) as well as detailed information on Feng Shui, the ancient Chinese geo-manufacturing process. The article doesn't mention anything about the intricate glueless and nailless joinery which was so popular in Chinese furniture.

When the people started to learn to cultivate their land, they began making furniture and eventually moved into permanent settlements. The oldest known furniture pieces in Europe originate from a stone-age village around 2100 BC located in Scotland. The Steinzeit farmers lived in huts that had turf and whalebone roofs. They also constructed stone furniture for indoor use such as beds and cupboards.

Egyptians lived in huge comfortable homes that had lots of bright rooms, with floors and walls. The wealthy Egyptians resided in homes with wooden furniture like tables, beds, desks and chests to store their belongings however they utilized head-made wooden pieces instead of pillows to store their belongings. People living in the ordinary lived in houses made of mud. They could have spent their nights sleeping on the hot roof, but they performed the majority of their work outdoors due to the temperatures. Furniture was easy for those who were poor and average Egyptians were sitting on brick benches amidst the walls. They also used wood shavings or wooden sticks to the walls for storage of things.

Even in lavish furniture in the past in Greece it was a necessity. The Greeks stored items in wooden boxes or put them up on walls using wooden sticks. There was also an armoire to display expensive cups, and people sitting in chairs (which could be used as beds) and sofas were wooden frames , with fabrics and mats or rugs.

The wealthy Romans were able to enjoy luxury items like mosaics and glass panes for windows (in areas that were colder than the empire) and even the central heat known as the hypocaust. The rich had extremely extravagant furniture, that was beautifully tapered and sculpted. They ate on sofas; oils lamps served to light and wall art inside their homes, which were called murals. For instance, people living in the slums of Romans were able to afford very basic and basic furniture.

The life was rough and tough even for the wealthy Saxons and their furnishings were quite basic. In most cases, there was just one room that was shared by all in the Saxon hall. Thanes and his followers slept in beds that were stuffed with mattresses and pillows, whereas the most poor people slept on the floor. There isn't much information on Saxon furniture, however, such as tables and beds made of wooden they is likely that it was massive and simple. The upper class Saxons prefer tapestries on their walls however, in windows they did not have glass panes in the halls of Thane.

Then, we realized that the wealthy person was able to afford better furniture throughout the yearsmostly European as well as African countries, with the exception of Britain. Do we continue with that 16th century?

Rich Saxons as well as their entire family resided in one hall. The huge hall remained in late in Middle Ages, but the Lord's room was over it. This room was referred to as"the solar room. The Lord lay in a tent with curtains to provide modesty as well as to block drafts. Other members of the household of the lord sleep in the huge hall, including his servants. At one or both ends of the grand hall the hall had a chimney, as well as an open fireplace. However, chimneys were lavish in the Middle Ages.

Medieval furniture was essential and chairs were scarce in the homes of wealthy familiesthe majority of people sat on benches or stools. People who were wealthy also had tables as well as large chests, which doubled as beds. The wealthiest families owned silky tapestries or linen that was painted and it wasn't only to decorate the home, it also helped keep drafts away.

At the time of 16th-century, items were designed to be more comfortable for the wealthy. Furniture was more plentiful than they were in earlier Middle Ages but still relevant. In the case of a luxurious home the furniture was constructed of oak and had massive large furniture. Furniture of the 16th century was thought to last for a long time and your kids and grandkids were required to have the furniture. The comfortable beds are more common and more people of middle class are sleeping on mattresses made of feathers instead of the more difficult ones. Chairs were common however they were expensive as ministers and children used to sit on benches and stools even in the posh house.

Glass windows became more widespread, however those who were poor required linen strips that were soaked into lens oils. The 16th century saw the introduction of chimneys. also were an option, but they became more well-known.

The walls were constructed with oak paneling in the rich Tudor Houses to keep drafts out. Many people slept with curtains in four-poster beds in order to minimize drafts. There were wallpapers that were in use from the 15th century. However, they were expensivewealthy people also hung tapestries or painted towels over their windows.

There was no change to the disadvantaged furniture in the 16th century. they lived in small dwellings that had a room or two and did not smoking in a crevice on the wall that was stubbled. Floors are made of soil and furniture, which included chairs, stubs and a table and wooden containers, was incredibly tiny. We were sleeping on mattresses lined by straw, or with thistledown, and lay on clothes that were spread over a room with wood.

Wood Furniture

The history of woodworking was based on the kinds of woods that were that were found in the field prior to the invention of export and transport provided the craftsman with exotic wood. Wood is classified into three fundamental kinds:

Tight-grained hardwoods derived from broadleaf tree,

Coniferous softwoods

Human-made materials like plain wood or MDF. Common furniture like chairs and tables is constructed from solid wood, and the manual as well as other table items made by humans are utilized by cabinet and fixture makers.

As culture developed through the years, the capabilities of humans were able to improve. Advanced woodworking techniques as well as techniques and designs were taught and woodworking became a form of art. Marquetry, parquetry and carpentry woodcarving, architecture, and parquetry are just a few of the essential abilities. These are all connected to the beauty and artistic quality of woodworking.

The woodworking sector has experienced a variety of shifts in recent times. It is possible to conclude that woodworking isn't just an "professional occupation" but also seen as a historical event in itself.

The tale continues to the furniture it was before bed (a drop-down table or fall-down pad that hangs at one end , which we could fold and then store in the vertical position against a wall or in a closet) or sofas and transform futons. The appearance and style are increasingly added to furniture and are then a hallmark to any furniture, which is the case with modern designs. Furniture designed for the wealthy got more comfortable and elegant towards the end of the 17th century. It was typically constructed from walnut or cowboy and was painted in new ways. Furniture was filled with small pieces of expensive wood, which was placed over cheaper wood. The wood was then sculpted then the mother wood of Perl filled in the hollow. Lacking was also used to make the KJrich furniture. Pieces of furniture were lacquered with brilliant shades.

There were various pieces of furniture that came out with drawers being more common while grandfather clocks gained popularity and the bookcase came into use later in the century. The seats were bigger thanks to upholstery and the first sleeves came to the market in this area.

The wealthy and rich purchased expensive furniture with upholstered upholstery during the 18th centurySome of which were decorated or even incubated. Clocks and armoires became more popular, but furniture was still scarce and basic for the less fortunate.

The 19th century was the first time in history manufacturing furniture in mass quantities. This resulted in a less expensive product as well as a dramatic drop in standards for design. The most vulnerable people have had to sleep on heaps of strokes because they couldn't pay for beds.

Gas cookware became popular around the turn into the century of 20thcentury however, because they could not warm the space they were used to they were able to spend most of their time in front of the fireplace, either in the living room or in the family room. The rise in living standards meant that more than one space could be properly decorated. Modern design and furniture called Art Deco was developed in the 1920s and 1930s. Instead of the wavy curves that were characteristic of the previous Art Nouveau, it used geometric forms. The term Art Deco comes from a 1925 show in Paris known as to be the International Exhibition of Decorative Arts. In the early 20th period, Britain became a prosperous society and the cost of furniture increased for common people.

Woodworking is the construction manufacturing, carving or manufacturing process that uses wood.

Wood was among the first materials used by humans, along with the mud, stone as well as animal organs. The microwear analysis of the instruments made of stone used by Neanderthals from Muster shows that many of them were employed to make with wood. The growth of civilisation was closely associated to the growth of new abilities in the use of the materials.

Chapter 11: Safety Precautions

When it comes down to woodworking taking safety precautions is vital to you to stay safe from injury. It is because when you work you are dealing with a range of tools and machinery. In order to avoid injuries, safety should be the top priority for everyone's thoughts. When working with wood, every hand tool such as portable power equipments, portable power tools and machines are used for a variety of purposes and each comes with its own risks in the event of misuse. Every person should be knowledgeable about their usage and their maintenance in order to guarantee safety. There are some fundamental guidelines to adhere to in order to remain secure. Some of the most crucial ones are described below:

* It is recommended to only make use of woodworking equipment that you know

and have been taught to operate in a correct and safe manner.

* For machines that have just been purchased, take the time to read the manual thoroughly and make sure you are aware of the entire instruction before you use any tool or machine.

Wear safety gear when working and make sure you have them in place until you leave the workshop.

* It is also important to be careful to wear the right clothes, avoiding loose fitting clothes since they may get caught in certain machines.

- Stay clear of the workshop if are intoxicated by any alcohol or other substances.

It is recommended to remove power before making changes to a blade or bit on an electric tool.

* Make use of one extension cord, as it forces you to change the cord between tool and tool before you use it. This allows you to be sure to unplug and plug the power whenever you move between tools.

Make sure you are always using sharp bits and blades because that a dull tool for cutting can be a deadly tool.

Before starting any cutting make sure you check for screws, nails and other metal.

Woodworking power tools are made in a manner that you must always be working against the cutter, and it should be kept in mind.

Another important point is to never touch a blade to take off cut offs, rather be patient until your blade stops moving.

Avoid distractions of any kind during work, since distracting your attention while using tools or machinery will result in catastrophe.

Importantly, ensure that you keep the floor and work area clear of spills of oil, clutter and wood scraps.

Be responsible enough to make sure you use the right equipment and tools for the job . Avoid using a tool or attachment to an equipment that is not specifically designed specifically for the task.

Before you plug into a machine, be sure to check the switch is off position and the switch that turns off is in the reach of.

If your machine doesn't sound as it should, emits an unusual smell or smoke is visible, you must immediately shut off the machine and examine for any issues before attempting to use it again.

Make sure to keep your fire extinguisher in a safe place.

*Before starting work, examine your work space for any unsafe conditions and take the necessary steps to remedy them.

Avoid any unsafe hand or hand position as a sudden slip could cause injury to your hand.

Do not leave any machine in operation without being watched.

Chapter 12: Techniques For Cutting Dovetails

If you now have an understanding of what mortises as well as Tenons are, this chapter will examine how you can develop your knowledge. We'll take a examine what dovetail joints are typically used for, and then most importantly, how you can construct one of your own. Similar to the other topics that were previously discussed in this guide so far, building a dovetail joint is sure require some time to master and practice, but once you've mastered the fundamental mortise and tenon joints which were covered in the previous chapter, it's certain that building a dovetail joint will be an easy task.

What is what is a Dovetail Joint?

We have already covered this earlier in this chapter instead of having to describe in words the dovetail joint like, it's better to provide the reader with an image of it.

A picture for a dovetail joints may be found below.

As you can tell from the image above the dovetail joint is like the mortise or tenon joints we examined previously in chapter. This is due to the fact that the dovetail joint features an intricate mortise and Tenon joint design. Dovetails aren't just appealing to the eye, they're also extremely durable as mortises and tenons. What makes these joints distinctive and attractive is the fact that they don't require screws or nails for them to be robust and durable.

Discussion on terminology

Before we go over exactly what you need to do when creating a dovetail joint it is necessary to be able to talk about the terms used in dovetails. There are two kinds of boards that you'll work to create dovetail joints, and the two kinds of boards are referred to by"tail out" and "pin-out" "tail out" board and the "pin out" board. Although it might be difficult to determine the difference between these two boards but it's simple to identify what's which when you think of the tail of a dove (or any bird's tail). The piece of wood that flares greater than another is referred to as the tailboard, and the one with the pins that are straighter are referred to as the pinboard. Below is a picture to clarify these aspects:

The Dovetail Jig

The next aspect of the language that we must discuss and be aware of prior to constructing our dovetail joint. It's called the dovetail Jig.

The dovetail jig is observed above. As you can observe there are ridges inside the jig. They constitute the grooves which permit the wood to cut through without breaking through. This is in stark contrast to the normal mortise and tenon joint in which the mortise joint totally eliminates itself to create space for the joint which will perfectly fit inside. The final result that the joint produces may be observed in the following image.

How to Utilize the Dovetail Jig

If you've now looked at the dovetail jig it would be useful to know how to utilize it. First, ensure that you set the tooth of your dovetail tool to the size you would like for the dovetail joint. It's crucial to ensure your teeth have an at a similar distance apart. If not, the joint will look unclean. After that, place the wood on top of the jig. Turn the machine off once you've measured everything, and are confident that your measurements are correct. Put the wood into the jig, taking care that your hands are kept away from the jig and to the lower part of the piece until it is in contact with to the top of jaws of the jig. Switch off the jig and then make adjustments to the teeth such they're opposite of the wood you've just put in the jig. If you had used pins previously, you're going to need to switch to the tails. If you take everything out properly and you'll find that the tails and pins are snug and fit togetherafter giving them a good jiggle and maybe a smack with mallets or two.

If the thought of purchasing more tools does not sound at all appealing If you are not sure, then consider making your own dovetails from scratch. This may be appealing to some woodworkers as they believe that there's more authenticity when dovetails are made by hand. If you're considering doing this, you'll be required to ensure you've made two fences one for the tails of a dovetail and another to hold the pins of the dovetail. This alone will take a lot of practice on either the circular or table saw whichever one you decide to purchase. You'll need to ensure that you're using what's referred to as a rip knife for this task, as this will give the top of your board the smooth surface you're seeking. When you are moving the wood toward the rip blade it's a good option to turn the piece over and make the dovetail cuts on both sides of the board prior to making cutting the following cut. This will ensure that the cuts are identical. Once you've completed making pins on one piece of wood and tails on the opposite part of the wood by using the saw, you will be able to connect the two pieces of wood together. Also, it should be emphasized that creating dovetails with your hands is likely need a considerable amount of practice however when you put your heart to it, there's nothing can't be achieved.

Chapter 13: Adhesives

While there are approximately 1500 adhesive products available within the U.S., less than 12 are suitable for use in woodworking. Before diving into specific types of adhesives it's important to comprehend how glue connects wood parts. It is essential to understand some of the chemical structure of wood as well as how adhesives connect to these elements during the bonding process. Wood is a complex mix of organic and water-based chemicals.

The majority of the board is made up of hemicelluloses, cellulose , and lignin. These components form the wood's structural matrix and give it robustness, durability, and flexibility. In the rest, 5 percent in dry wood is made up of essential oils and tannins, as well as gums, sugars, resins and colorants. This chemical mix of extractives creates wood's smell as well as color and resistance to decay.

Once an adhesive is applied to the wood surfaces surrounding it and the pieces are securing to the wood, the structural elements that make up the structure of wood get bonded through the bonding process. The adhesive fluid initially is absorbed into the wood, and its polymer particles are bonded with the wood fibers that form the structural. The adhesive's polymer particles meld or come together, covering the fibers of the structure and then become solid, thereby locking them mechanically.

Thermosetting glues such as urea-formaldehyde epoxy, and resorcinol are cured by an chemical reaction, usually when two elements have been incorporated, while thermoplastic adhesives such as yellow and white glues cure through evaporation. When either type of glue has dried the thin layer between the two wood surfaces serves as a bridge to keep the boards in place.

Polyvinyl Acetates

Yellow and white glues are probably the most commonly and popular glues used in woodworking nowadays. Both are polyvinyl alcohol (PVA) adhesives which are available in three main varieties: craft white glue as well as yellow aliphatic resin and cross-linking PVA. All three have an optimally balanced set of properties which make them ideal to glue wood. They're easy to use and have a quick grab, aren't harmful and work in all situations for wood-gluing. Furthermore, the liquid adhesives will deteriorate in the event of freezing. But, PVA adhesives do are not very resistant to creep and should never be used for structures, such as beams for load bearing, without some kind of mechanical fixing, such as nail or screws.

Resorcinol and Urea-Formaldehyde

Resorcinol formaldehyde and urea-formaldehyde are used most commonly to bond wood when strong water-, creep-, and bonds are required. Urea-formaldehyde (UF) adhesive In some instances, is sometimes referred to as plastic glue, is a single-part powder. It is a mixture of resins and dry hardeners that, if kept dry, can be stored for a long time. The addition of water helps to melt the chemical and activate the adhesive. The time between mixing and blending is quite long. But the viscosity of the activated glue gradually increases until, about an hour later, the glue is too thick to use. After curing, UF adhesives create structural bonds, and the tan glueline is virtually invisible when the wood is light colored. Panels of plywood made from hardwood and beams that carry loads inside are often joined with UF adhesives. However, it's not 100% water-resistant.

Resorcinol formaldehyde is extremely strong that is incredibly resistant to solvents and, when properly cured, will withstand prolonged periods of immersion in water, making them perfect for marine applications. The RF glues are two-part sets. Part one contains the resorcinol resin that is liquified with alcohol ethyl whereas the second part is composed of paraformaldehyde powdered. The components that have been measured are mingled to activate the adhesive. However, careful mixing is necessary to avoid lumps.

Working with RF and UF adhesives could cause health issues and should be done in a ventilated area wear a mask and break whenever you can. Both emit formaldehyde gas.

Epoxy

They are strong and durable, with incredible gap-filling ability, capability to join components that are difficult to bond and their water-resistant properties they are definitely the best-performing adhesives available in the woodworking world. Epoxy is a combination of an amine hardener as well as epoxy resin. In general, the components of resin and hardener are combined to trigger the adhesive and initiate the curing process, which works through chemical reaction instead of solvent evaporate. The exact percentages of blending are vital; too high a percentage of either ingredient is likely to affect the bonding power. Because of the absence of solvent, epoxy has incredible ability to fill in gaps.

Chapter 14: Important Things To Remember When Setting Up A Woodshop

For someone who is just beginning to learn the woodshop should likely be located in the garage, basement or even a shed. The space isn't much of an issue for the beginner because the use of big equipment isn't common. But as time passes the skills develop and big tools must be employed. This is the time that woodworkers may need to create a new layout of the shop from scratch, or remodel an existing space to make it more efficient space. Create a workspace that is both functional and comfortable. In addition, you should take into consideration space and layout to ensure a smooth workflow.

In designing a shop there are three fundamental items that a woodworker should be aware of:

Layout your layout to maximize functionality and effectiveness

Be aware of noise and comfort when deciding on features

Draw a rough layout of the area on paper.

Be sure the woodshop is properly lit, which lets you be able to see what you're doing. This will give you a clear overview of the work that is taking place on a particular project. A good number of power outlets is required to prevent extension cords cluttering up the shop. Make sure the outlets can accommodate the power required by the tools being used in the woodshop.

Reduced noise is an important consideration when planning a woodshop, particularly if it's located on the bottom of the. You should consider using rubber feet for your tables and equipment as well as insulating the air ducts and ceiling and disassociating the wallboards from ceiling joists to lessen the sound and vibration.

The flooring is one part of the woodshop often neglected. There are a variety of instances where the concrete floor can be very hard for woodworkers' feet and tools. It is recommended to put mats made of rubber to safeguard anything that may get into the flooring in the shop.

One of the things that build up in every wooden shop or workshop is dust. Therefore, it's a good idea to invest in shop equipment such as dust collection HVAC and heating and air plumbing. This will significantly increase the security and ease of use in the woodshop.

Verify that the woodshop's door is large enough to hold the project you'll must take away after its completion. There's nothing more frustrating than getting furniture in the woodshop that is stuck because doors don't have enough width for you to remove it after you've finished.

Be sure to have an sufficient ceiling height that will permit you to work with wooden boards of different heights. It will be a challenge to turn over an entire sheet of plywood which is 10 feet tall when your ceiling is just 8 feet. If you're planning your shop from scratch, make sure you have at minimum the height of 10 feet in order to accommodate the various sheet wood sizes that are common.

Install peg boards on the bare walls that surround the shop. Peg board panels help in maximising space and make it easy to access the tools typically used in a construction. There is a large assortment of hand tools on a peg boards, including sets of chisels, screw driver sets mallets, hammers and lots more.

Make sure you have specialized storage cabinets to keep the larger hand tools in order and out of sight. There's nothing that is more dangerous than a huge circular saw stored in the woodshop. The cabinets are designed to also be used to store smaller items to keep them from getting lost during work.

When building your woodshop be aware that the majority of woodworking novices don't have the luxury of having a shop that is spacious enough and the tools they'll ever need. There will be sacrifices and compromises However, proper planning can make the entire process enjoyable and easy.

Chapter 15: Diy Project Plans

There are several woodworking tasks you can experiment with by yourself as a beginner . These projects can implement at home or in the in your garden.

1. Garden Furniture Designs

Chair

You can create yourself a Patio chair to sit within the backyard.

and Materials and Materials

Cedarwood (pinewood or fir the spruce)

(12 inches) miter saw

Drill

Table saw

Clamps

Tape measures

Jigsaw

Kreg jig

Orbital sander

Impact driver

Carpenters square

Pencil

Straight edge

Sandpaper

2x4 Boards, 1x4 Boards, 2x6 Board, 1x6 Board, Wood Screws, Wood Glue, Wood Putty

Step 1: First, cut the legs. Cut the most of them with miter saw.

Measure the measurement from the bottom of the piece and make a mark. Create another mark on the measurement of five and a half inches. Make another measurement of one-half inch to form the notch to accommodate the 2x6 board which connects with the two legs in front. A 2x6 board measures 5 1/2 inches in width as well as 1 1/4 inches in thickness.

Step 2: Take out the notches using an Jigsaw

Connect all of the feet to the front of the two-by-6 board. Use the carpenter's squaring tool to ensure that the legs fit in the notch with precision. Make sure to drill the holes prior to splitting the wood. Apply wood glue to the joints, then screw it in.

Step 3. Fix the armrests of the chair.

The chair should be turned upside down and apply three screws and wood glue to secure the armrest support to the legs in front.

Rear Legs

Cut the legs of the rear in a 15 degree angle. Secure the legs with a clamp as you align them. Measure 12 inches from the back on the back leg. The rear leg should be placed at the point, then align it so that it is aligned with to the highest point of your armrest, and the leg is firmly resting upon the floor.

Fix the legs on the rear. Measure the table's surface. Fix the support in place and secure it with screws and glue on the other side. Front of rear leg, as well as that lower edge of the support must be in line, and the support board must be laid straight, with 90 degrees of angle.

Seat Supports

Put three-seat support on both ends and in the middle. The front side of the boards should be cut in 90 degrees, while the other at 15 degrees. By using a couple of screws, you can fix your legs onto the outer supports. Be sure that the board is level with the ground and is resting securely on the support board at the rear.

Backrest Supports

Cut the backrest support at 15 degrees at each end, with another two thirty degree angles to be cut at the top of it to create a round shape. Set the backrest support in place to complete the frame.

Step 4: Make the Chair and Seat

The back and seat could be made of 1x4 board, which is typically 3 1/2 inches in width with a thickness of 3/4 inches. Each board is spaced with 1/4 inch spacer. To make them fit, use table saws to narrow the size of one or two boards, if needed but be sure to drill them prior to. Begin from the front and work your way to behind the seats. Then create a 1/4 overlap over the front of the board.

Form and attach armrests

Apply a paint container to the side of armrests. With a miter saw and a 45-degree angle, cut to the back of the armrest. Utilize wood glue and screws to attach the armrest to the top of the side.

Wood Putty

Put wood putty into the screw holes , making sure that the screw holes are not counter-sunk. Once the putty has dried remove it using an orbital sander. Make sure to not put any extra putty on the armrests. You can finish your chair using any stain you want.

Table

To build a table for your garden You must follow these steps:

First step: cut the Lap Joints

The first step is to construct your "X's". Cut the lap joints starting with the two edges. Cut a few more between them so that you don't cut the entire length of the hole.

Step 2: Assemble Legs

Make sure the cut lap joints match and join them using wooden screws as well as glue. Be cautious not to join the lap joints with the wrong side of wood.

Cut and sand the legs to prevent them from breaking off the edges. Utilize a circular saw to remove the small sharp edge.

Step 3: Build a Frame for the top

Take the legs apart and create the top. You'll require for the Kreg Jig as pocket holes are the primary components. Make them fixable using the 2 12 " Pocket holes.

Step 4 4. Attach the Trim to the Frame

The table can be trimmed with 2x4's, so that they can be glued to the edges. Join the trim pieces, leaving an extra 3/4 " area to attach the 1x4's. To make this process easy make sure you add some scrap 1x4" pieces underneath the frame. Make sure to keep the trim pieces out of sight however, work on an even surface.

Step 5: Assemble Table

With wood glue and screws connect the legs with the frame of your table. Join the 4x4 board to each leg before fixating the top frame with the Kreg Jig.

You can choose to make patterns on your table , but in the event that you don't, sand and complete your table.

Bench

This is how to construct the garden bench.

and Materials and Materials

1x3x6" Board

2-inch exterior deck screws

Exterior Wood Filler

Sandpaper

2x12x10' board

3-inch exterior deck screws

Exterior Wood Stain

Exterior Wood Exterior Wood

Jigsaw

Drill

Miter saw

Circular saw

Cut List

2x12 Seat One @ 42 inches

2x12 Stringer - 1 @ 30 inches

2x12 Legs - 2 @ 16 1/2 inches

1x3 Trim - 2 @ 42 inches

Step 1. Cut the boards using the cut list.

Cut the 2x12 boards with miter saws to create the leg, seat as well as stringer piece. Cut the trim pieces using 1x3 boards.

Step 2. Mark the legs' legs with a line.

Take measurements of the leg pieces and draw a line 4 inches on each edge of the lower edge. Add 5 1/2 inches to the bottom of each leg , centered them in the width of each board. Draw an outline of the lines and sketch the cutouts of triangles.

Step 3. Mark the leg's details

Take a jigsaw, and cut the outline you created in step 2. Utilize a circular saw to cut the lines. Finally, employ the jigsaw for cutting the notch's tip.

Step 4: Measure the stringer

Take 3 1/4 inches off the length of the stringer using the circular saw.

Step 5: Insert the stringer inside the legs.

Place wood glue on the bottom of the stringer 2x12. The board should be placed at the intersection between the legs, with the trimmed edge aligned with the top side of every leg. Drill two pilot holes through the legs until the ends of the stringer. Drill three-inch wood screws through the pilot holes, allowing them to get to the stringer.

Step 6: Take your seat with the Framework

Install wood glue on the tops of the stringer and leg. Set the seat board directly with its sides on the base flush with a similar spread of about 4 inches from both ends. Install two pilot holes into the seat in order to reach each leg, and three pilot holes to reach the stringer away from the seat. Install deck screws of 3 inches in the legs as well as in the stringer that passes through the seat.

Step 7: Create the seat trim

The ends of the trim pieces of 1x3 approximately 1 1/2 inches away from their top edges. Follow the markings to secure the bottom corner to the miter saw at a 45 degrees .

Step 8 Connect the Seat Trim

Apply wood glue to both sides of your seat. Attach the trim edge to the highest part of the seating, putting the corners clipped down. Create three pilot holes in the trim pieces. Using two-inch screws, join the trim pieces to the seat. Use wood fillers made of exterior grade to fill screws. Smooth the screws and use wood stain. Use after it dries.

Flowerpot

This is how you can make your own flowerpot.

Materials and tools

Jigsaw

Block plane

Drill

Table saw

Cedarwood

Step 1: Cut the four panels.

Cut the panel pieces in half and cut one edge off of each corner piece. Make use of a jigsaw to slice the panels. Keep in mind that one piece on each panel is 11/16 inches thinner than the counterpart on the opposite side.

Set three pieces of panel (two straight and one tapered) on a piece of plywood, separating them using 1/8 inch spacers. Install guide strips to hold the plywood pieces in the right place. Cut each cleat shorter than the desired length by about a hair's width. Make sure the cleat is fixed by 1/4 inch.

Step 2: Put together the box

Install the planter, but first make sure you slant the edges of the tapered, narrower part of each panel with an incline plane that is just a little less than 90 degrees. Join the panels using thin wedges as well as a band clamp and then insert Deck screws through the top corners of the planter.

Then, drill a series of pilot holes 1/16 inches through the corners of the planter and then insert a final nail in the holes, keeping out the panel that is adjacent.

Use glue on the joint after taking off the screws and band clamp. Set the box up with the screws, and then drive in the nails. Allow the nailheads to penetrate into the surface to be able to hold outside grade wood filler. Cut and then screw three pieces of the bottom into the desired position.

Step 3: Design the cap

Make the caps pieces smaller in half and create pilot holes for the final nails will be placed to secure them. The pilot holes should be not too far away from cutting miter lines. Apply glue and nail to the fullest extent.

Cut the miters off the L-shaped pieces then use a clamp to keep the cap while you create tiny holes in the cap for nails. Remove the clamp, apply glue over the miters, then reclaim and put it back together. assembly.

Make a slight plane on the tops of the cleats using a block plane in order to bring them to a level. Set the cap in a position where it is evenly overhangs, and then drill pilot holes into the cleats. Remove the cap then rub glue on the cleats and then nail to the cap. When the glue is dry then set the nailheads, and apply wood filler. Use 120 or 220-grit aluminum oxide to sand the surface. Then you can put your flower in the flowerpot.

Swing bed

Here's how to build the swing bed

and Materials and Materials

Miter Saw

Jig Saw

2"Finish" Nails

1 1/4" Finish Nails

Wood Stain

Measurement Tape Measurer

Finish Nailer

4 Eye Screws

Wood Glue

Sand Paper

Wood Filler

11.11 pieces from 1 3 8 clear pine

three pieces that are 1 8 inches 8' clear pine

Three pieces from 1 3 8" knotty pine

two pieces 3 8 framing lumber

1 . Piece of"'" x 4 8" clear pine

A piece made of two 4 8" framing lumber

Note that all joints have butt joints. Apply wood glue to all joints.

Step 1: Create the frame.

Make the bed frame using 1x8's by using 2" finishing nails to the joints. Incorporate an additional frame into the makeup. Utilize 2x4's to make the frame bigger enough to fit eyes screws. Be sure that you have the top of your 2x4's are exactly the same height as the bottom of your frame. Utilize the two" nails to attach onto the frames. Make use of 2x3's for the front and back, and ensure that its top is at the same level that it is on top of your 2x4's.

Cut 6 39" wide pieces of 1x3 knotty pine to make the slats, and then arrange equally on the outside of your bed frame. This will support this bed frame.

Step 2. Create the Posts

Create four posts using clear pine 1x3 for each corner. Create the post using two pieces by gluing them on the other edge.

The second piece should be placed on top of the glue edge to create the "L" shape. Make sure that the edges line up precisely. Utilize two" nails to join the two pieces. Next, use 1 1/4 nail and glue to join the corner of the post.

Step 3: Repair the rails

Take the rails off when you've finished putting all four posts. These are the horizontal pieces which will connect the posts. Join the back rails first, after which you can attach the sides rails.

The armrests need additional cutting. So, using 1x3 pieces and cut the pieces into length. Make use of a jigsaw for an opening that allows it to fit over an armrest's back.

After cutting the pieces, nail and glue them into the correct position. Attach 1x3 trim on all 4 sides on the bottom of the swing by using 1/4 " nails and glue.

Then , add the top support to the back, and then the inner rail support. You can use 1x4 for the top while 1x3 is used for middle support.

Step 4 Step 4: Fill Holes and stain

Fill in all holes with wood putty, then smooth the corners with fine sandpaper. Then , apply the stain you like.

Step 5: Repair the Eye Screws

Make sure the eye screws are tightened when the setup is dry. The rope will pass through them, and will hold the swing. Take a measurement of one" from the top of the post then 1 1/4" upwards from the bottom until you reach your middle lower trim piece. Drill a hole in the post and insert the screw for eye into.

Eye screws are required for hanging the swing, but make certain that you've put the screws into the ceiling's joists. After that, you can put in pillows and mattresses.

Compost storage

Materials and tools

Bow saw

Solid wooden pallets (four)

Wooden stakes made of sturdy material (six)

Spade or Rake

Strong wire

Sledgehammer

Step 1 Step 1: Step 1: Level the soil

Clean up the area using an rake or spacer to make the ground level or, if necessary. The bin should be set on the soil that is not. To stop rats from getting in the area, put a foundation made consisting of wire from chickens.

Step 2: Repair the pallet

Place a pallet on its long side to form the back side that will be the front of your composter. Put a stake through each of the layers on each end and secure them to the ground using an sledgehammer in a distance of 20-30cm.

Step 3: Attach stakes to the ground.

To construct the sides you can use the two last pallets to make an angle with respect to the previous one. Be sure that the corners are secure so that compost doesn't get in. Set them up with stakes at each corner as in the second step.

Step 4: Secure the pallets using wire

Connect all the pallets at each corner to help stabilize the structure. Utilize a bow saw to reduce off the tops of the stakes. Then, you can create gates with the remaining pallet by connecting it to the top of the right side pallet. The compost is now ready.

2. Indoor furniture design

Children's Bed

and Materials and Materials

- Dovetail Saw
- Table Saw
- Miter Saw
- 1x6x6' (x1)
- 1x4x8' (x3)
- 2x3x8' (x4)
- 2x4x8' (x2)
- 4x4x8' (x1)
- Caps for 4x4 Wood Caps (x4) Caps (x4)
- Wood Glue
- Kreg Jig
- 2"Wood Screws"
- 2 1/2 2 1/2
- 1/4" Plywood 4'x4' (x1)
- Drill
- Tape Measure

1 1/4 1 1/4" pocket hole screws

Random Orbital Sander

Nail Gun

Decor Wood Caps Caps

1. To build the bed for a toddler, cut 4x4

Make four 24-" post pieces from regular 4x4 lumber

Step 2: Make the Headboard and Footboard

Make two 2x3 pieces up to 24" in length to make both the sides of your headboard. Create two pocket holes at the edges of the 2x3 boards. Create a wide notch with one quarter " thickness as well as 1/4 " width on the middle of each of the boards using the table saw. This is to make an 1/8 " plywood. Then, divide one 1/4 " plywood into 19 1/2 " by 12 1/2 ". Apply wood glue to the joint connections of 2x3 and an 4 " notch. Slide the plywood into the notch. Use the 2 1/4 " pockets holes to connect the 2x3 boards. Repeat this process to create the footboard.

Step 3. Connect the Headboard and Footboard panel to the 4x4 posts.

On each 4x4 post take a measurement to mark the the post 4" at the base. Make use of 2-1/2 " pocket holes to attach your headboard to posts. Make sure the headboard is at the four" mark starting from the bottom, and is adjacent to the other side. This is the case for the footboard. Step 4: Make the back of the bed.

Similar to step 2 Cut 2x3 boards up to fifty-three " in length. Then cut two pieces of 2x3 to nine" long. When you have finished the 2x3 boards, create pockets, and then make use of a table saw to create an 1/8 " hole at the center. Cut the quarter " plywood and insert it in the notch then utilize two half " pockets holes screws fix each of four panels. Connect the finished panel to the post using two half " pockets holes screws. Place the back panel one 1/2 " from the corner on the inside of the post. elevate the top 4" of it off the lower part on the posts.

5. Fix the back 2x4 mattress support

Cut a piece of 2x4 up to 50 1/4" in length. Then, make two pockets on each end. Utilizing 2 1/2 pocket hole screws, connect the posts to the 2x4 post and make sure that it is four" from the base on the posts.

Step 6: Make the front of the bed

The front panel for the bed is built using steps 2, 4, and 5 using 2x3 boards. The front panel measures approximately 28" long. Create pocket holes only on the area which joins it to the post of the 4x4 and put it back 1 1/2 " as on the other side. Join the mattress support 2x4 4" by pressing the button. After installation, attach the front panel against the mattress support 2x4 using two" wooden screws.

Step 7: Place Mattress Frame Slats

The mattress support is now made up of 1x4 frame-slat boards. Cut nine pieces down between 27 and 9" in length, and then arrange them on supports made of 2x4. There should be a gap of 12 " between the slats of 1x4 and secure the boards to 2x4 support using nail guns.

Step 8: Decorate 4x4 Wood Cap

Make use of decorative wood caps on the posts of 4x4 either using nail guns or wood glue. Take how far between your front and the post, then cut one piece of 1x6 and secure it in place with two" wood screws. This will create an edging board that covers the frame slats.

To conceal visible pocket holes make a cut in a 3/8 wooden dowel rod up to two" inches in length. Douse it in wood glue and place it in the hole. Utilize a dovetail sander to cut any dowels sticking out, then sand it using a random orbital sander.

Chapter 16: What to Set Up Your Workbench

A workbench has been described as the curved stone of the woodshop. It has the history that is as long as the woodworking process itself. Workbench models from the early days have been discovered dating to more than 2,000 years ago.

The woodworkers of the early Rome developed the basic design of benches, constructing benches with simple stops that let them keep pieces of wood in place. Before that craftsmen were required to stand their work while cutting or shaping it using one hand, while chopping or cutting using the other.

Improvements continued, but slowly nonetheless, and vises were added several centuries afterward. With each advancement, the workbench is now playing an increasingly important position within the workshop. It's no surprise that many consider the workbench the most important tool that a woodworker could own.

A great workbench will not have a direct role to play in the woodworking process-it will not cut or shape wood it, but the bench, along with its accessories also perform a vital function It lets you allow you to free your hands and move the work to allow you to shape, cut and drill form and finish it effectively.

In the past too, benches that were most popular have not met the ideal. With its huge single-plank top, the Roubo Bench of the 18th Century was a hit across Europe but it came with no tail vises or bench dogs to support an item; instead it was a task performed through a system of iron holdfasts as well as the leg vise was an option.

100 years after 100 years later, the American Shakers improved on the Roubo. The bench they built was a massive piece

that featured the top of a laminated as well as a bench system with pet holes as well as an L-shaped tail vise, as well as leg vise.

Its Shaker bench wasn't much different from the contemporary cabinetmaker's bench. The style of the bench has not been altered much from the beginning of the 19th century the only thing that has changed is its accessories and the method of assembly have changed.

Some even say that the real invention is the Ron Hickman's invention, the ubiquitous Workmate. It was developed in the 1960s and the Workmate changed the way that many people think about work outside spaces, since it provided certain of the clamping features of a typical workbench but with a an easily collapsible and portable design.

Although Workmate Workmate has found a place in workshops across the globe many woodworkers-both professional and amateur still prefer only a solid wood bench made of maple or beech.

Many times, they decide to build their ownbench, they believe that the effort and care they put into making the bench will reflect in their subsequent work. The next chapter explains how to build the modern workbench for cabinetmakers, and how to set up the vises and other accessories needed to transform a bench into a more adaptable workstation.

The bench is designed after the traditional bench used by cabinetmakers, constructed from solid maple. It comes with two vises that are thought to be common tools, a face vise at the left-hand side of the front of the bench as well as a tail vise with a dog block slide that is mounted on the opposite side.

You can purchase the plans for the bench and then order the materials yourself. You can also follow the steps in this chapter and build the bench that meets your requirements.

No matter which route you decide to take the workbench is constructed in three distinct stages that are the base, the top, and finally the clamping accessories like bench dogs, vises and hold-downs.

The top of the most benches are generally anywhere between 33 to 36 inches tall. The best height for you is determined using the measurement of the space between your hand and floor as you sit up straight with your arms to your sides.

Make sure your workbench is finished with two layers of an oil-based product, like tung oil. The products penetrate the surface and protect wood, but the surface can also be restored simply by scrubbing it using steel wool and recoating.

How do you construct the base

The foundation of a workbench usually consists of two rectangular fames joined with stretchers.

The frames are basically the same with each having the same foot, arm as well as two legs.

The left-hand arm of the frame can be about 3 inches more than the arm on the opposite side in order to offer additional support for your face-vise.

To build a bench, you can use 8/4 maple that is 1 3/4 inches thick after surface.

The arms, feet and legs are built from two pieces of wood, which are glued together. They are then trimmed to the proper size on the jointer as well as the planer.

If you'd like to build the base using mortise and Tenons, cut four-shouldered Tenons at the ends of the legs. Then, rout identical mortises into the arms and feet.

Tenons can also be cut at the ends of stretchers, and mortises are required for the legs.

The joint between the stretchers as well as the legs must be sturdy, but still flexible that they can be removed in the event that you need moving the bench.

So, the knockdown hardware that is designed to serve this purpose is typically employed to connect the leg stretchers.

The following pages will describe other methods for strengthening knockdown connections.

Utilizing rods with truss

Instead of using mortise and tenon joints , to make the base, try butt joints, which are strengthened by rods for truss.

Kits are available, and rods are loosened or tightened following installation to account for the movement of wood in response to fluctuations in humidity.

Rout grooves for rods to be inserted into the edges of the stretchers as well as the inner edges of the legs. The dimensions and depth of the channels should be the same as that of the rod's size.

Check the assembly of the base and mark the grooves on the arms and legs.

Make a hole in each mark and make the diameter the same as the rods' diameter; countersink the holes until you can push the nuts in a flush manner with the wood's exterior.

Install the base by placing the rods in the holes and grooves and then tightening the connections by using nuts and washers.

Line the grooves with an inlay of solid wood if you would like to cover the rods.

Utilizing machine bolts as well as wood blocks

To ensure the bond between the stretchers and the legs to strengthen the connection, glue a block of wood with the same thickness of the stock on the edges of stretchers.

The blocks increase the area of contact between the stretchers and legs.

When the glue is dry After the glue has dried, cut a tenon on the top of each stretcher. You will also need an identical mortise into the leg.

Connect the pieces, and drill two holes for machine bolts to go through the leg and the tenon inside the blocks. Countersink these holes.

You can make the connection quick by inserting the bolts in the holes, inserting washers and tightening nuts.

By using lag screws and dowels

Another method for strengthening a mortise or Tenon joint between the legs and stretchers.

Cut a 1 inch-diameter wood dowel into a length that is equivalent to the width of stretcher.

Then, drill a 1 inch hole in the stretcher approximately 1 1/2 inches away from the stretcher's end.

Make a hole to install a lag screw in the leg. Stop the drill once the bit gets to the hole in the stretcher. Countersink the hole until the screw head is in a straight line with the outside.

Install the stretcher's tenon into the mortise in the leg, then tap the dowel into the stretcher and then push the screw.

Pick a screw long enough to penetrate the dowel.

How to prepare your feet

1. Relieving feet

After you're happy with the fit of the components on the bottom, take them apart the legs and stretchers, and then remove the feet from the jointer.

Install a clamp onto the jointer's infeed table that will ensure that the guard is away from the way during the jointer is working.

Set both outfeed and infeed tables to a 1/16 inch cutting depth and clamp stop block to both tables to mark the beginning and the end of cutting.

To begin the first run begin by lowering the foot down onto the knives, making sure it is in line with the fence as well as the stop block on the feed table.

Feed the foot over cutting knives till it touches the stop block that is on the table for outfeed.

Make sure that both hands are well above the cutter's head.

Perform as many passes as needed to fill the recess. Lower the tables by 1/16 inch at a time, altering the stop blocks according to the need.

2. Installing adjustable levelers

To level a bench on the floor of a shop that is uneven Install adjustable levelers into the feet.

Each leveler is comprised of a T-nut as well as an end-of-thread with an edge made of plastic.

Make two holes in the lower part of the foot close to the two ends.

Create a hole with a diameter equal to the diameter of the T-nut, and its length should be slightly longer than the threaded portion.

Place the T-nuts in the holes, then screw them into the levelers.

After the bench has been set up, you can make adjustments to the levelers so that the bench is level.

How do you build the top

The most important aspects of a workbench is the flat top.

In the past the bench top would be made from solid beech or maple boards that were 12 inches wide as well as 2 inches in thickness.

Today, such slabs are difficult to find and bench top slabs are constructed using thin boards, layers plywood sandwiched between strips hardwood or plywood laminated strips wrapped in hardboard.

But edge gluing solid wood boards in a butcherblock style is a time-honored method.

Cut from 8/4 stock the boards are glued first, and then the slab is cut into length.

To reduce warping, arrange the pieces in a way that the grain on the other side is reversed.

Make sure that the face grain of all boards is in the same direction.

This will allow you to smooth the top surface of the slab.

Conclusion

After you have read all the information on how to begin woodworking I hope it has given you the desire to get started with the craft to express your artistic side or to use woodworking as a source of additional income. Woodworking is an extremely rewarding art which not only allows people to be more creative but also provides us with an opportunity to improve ourselves betterand make new and useful items.

It is the next thing to do starting a small woodworking project to start. Begin with a simple project you can use to decorate your home or small furniture before slowly getting into more difficult projects, such as larger-scale wood furniture or outdoor construction.

We thank you for your support and hope that you have fun with the woodworking project you've chosen to work on.

www.ingramcontent.com/pod-product-compliance
Lightning Source LLC
Chambersburg PA
CBHW071839080526
44589CB00012B/1058